More Praise for *The New Social Learning*

"Campfires and coffee machines have always embodied a secret sauce for informal learning and cultural richness, and social media has magnified that potential exponentially. Bingham and Conner have written a smart, useful guide for understanding both the possibilities and the pitfalls of this new and increasingly significant part of our world. Distinct from all the pop-culture commentary about the likes of Twitter and Facebook, this is a refreshingly sophisticated and studied analysis of what's really valuable in this arena and how to make the best use of it. A great handbook for our times."

David Allen
Author of *Getting Things Done* and *Making It All Work*

"Most workplace learning occurs not in the classroom, but through ongoing, daily social interactions with others. This new book from Bingham and Conner, complete with dozens of real-life examples and case studies, shows the myriad ways smart organizations are leveraging new technologies and strategies to support and sustain social learning at work."

Jane Bozarth
Author of *Social Media for Trainers, From Analysis to Evaluation,*
and *Better than Bullet Points*

"Want to thrive in today's world of constant change? Then read this book—a book of evocative stories about the power of social learning in organizations but these stories apply to us as individuals just as well. Read and enjoy and then adopt its wisdom."

John Seely Brown
Independent Co-Chairman, Deloitte's Center for the Edge
Former Chief Scientist, Xerox Corporation
and Director of Xerox Palo Alto Research Corp (PARC)
Co-author of *The Power of Pull: How Small Moves,
Smartly Made, Can Set Big Things in Motion*

"The New Social Learning is an absolutely fascinating exploration into how social media can change and is changing the workplace into knowledge organizations. Read this book! Your future success may depend on it."

Marshall Goldsmith

World-renowned executive coach

Author of *The New York Times* best-sellers *Mojo*

and *What Got You Here Won't Get You There*

"This book is both inspirational and at the same time pragmatic, as it explains how the new social learning can transform the workplace. Learning managers should be excited by the new possibilities of harnessing social media to facilitate social learning in their organizations."

Jane Hart

CEO, Centre for Learning & Performance Technologies (C4LPT)

"Enterprises around the world are recognizing that the way we work in a globally integrated business world is changing. This book is wonderfully written with practical advice on how to create a culture that can thrive in this environment by taking a people-centric approach to how we collaborate to get things done. While the internet and social tools can augment an individual's abilities, the stronger focus in this book is on how networks of individuals can redefine the way people learn and work together to foster a more flexible, collaborative, and participative environment. We are already seeing organizations that are embracing these changes outpace their competition."

Kristen Lauria

Vice President, Marketing & Channels

Lotus & Websphere Portal

IBM

"Finally, here is a book that extends the use of social media to the complex world of training and development. Bingham and Conner leverage their combined knowledge of organizations large and small to provide concrete strategies that will help your employees learn with greater speed and ease."

Alexandra Levit

Author of *New Job, New You: A Guide to Reinventing Yourself in a Bright New Career*

"Leaders making the greatest impact these days are open and relationship-oriented and support a culture of sharing while also maintaining command. This book provides an invaluable roadmap for how learning and social technology can accelerate that transformation."

Charlene Li, Author, *Open Leadership: How Social Technology Can Transform the Way You Lead*
Co-author, *Groundswell*

"As business leaders, we've been buzzing about the benefits of social media: keeping up with the rapid rate of change and the speed of innovation, knowledge sharing, informal learning, and employee engagement to name a few. We already know why we want social media. Conner and Bingham have finally told us how. They link clear business challenges to social media concepts without fixating on a particular tool. In a sea of social learning theory, this book provides business application for business results."

Anthony Loyd
Global Head, Learning & Development
Diversey, Inc.

"Learners are increasingly turning to social networking to share expertise and enhance the learning process. Tony Bingham and Marcia Conner provide a brilliant perspective on how organizations can design and harness the power of social learning."

Elliott Masie
Chair, The Learning CONSORTIUM

"In *The New Social Learning*, Bingham and Conner lay out a compelling case for learning's dramatic transformation and a roadmap for companies trying to harness it. This book is an obvious read for learning professionals and a smart read for the enlightened senior executive who is interested in creating a true learning culture."

Kevin Oakes
CEO, Institute for Corporate Productivity, Inc. (i4cp)

"This book shows how social media turns learning moments into an ongoing conversation where people can learn nonstop."

Garry Ridge
President & CEO, WD-40 Company

"In *The New Social Learning*, Tony Bingham and Marcia Conner provide a compelling case for embracing social media tools and strategies that make it possible for everyone to learn from everybody, anytime and anywhere. Rich with examples and perfectly timed, this eye-opening book is a must read for anyone involved in creating high-value learning for the knowledge-rich and increasingly digital workplace."

Marc J. Rosenberg, PhD
Consultant and educator in learning and e-learning
Author of *Beyond E-Learning*

"Learn from those adopting a new way of working: with people at the center."

Susan Scrupski
Executive Director, The 2.0 Adoption Council

"If you're interested in engaging stories, practical advice, and ideas on how to advance social learning in your organization, this is the book for you. Bingham and Conner meet you wherever you are in the journey and pragmatically offer everything from the theoretical underpinnings of social learning to how to use Twitter for customer support. Social learning is here now, and this book is an essential read for anyone in the learning profession."

Karie Willyerd
Co-founder, Future Workplace

The New Social Learning

The New Social Learning

A Guide to Transforming Organizations Through Social Media

Tony Bingham and Marcia Conner

Foreword by Daniel H. Pink

Alexandria, Virginia

Berrett–Koehler Publishers, Inc.
San Francisco
a BK Business book

15 14 13 12 11 10   1 2 3 4 5 6 7 8

Ordering Information

Quantity sales. Special discounts are available on quantity purchases by corporations, associations, and others. For details, contact the "Special Sales Department" at the Berrett-Koehler address above.

Individual sales. Berrett-Koehler publications are available through most bookstores. To order directly from Berrett-Koehler: Tel: (800) 929-2929; Fax: (802) 864-7626; www.bkconnection.com. To order directly from the American Society for Training & Development: Tel: (800) 628-2783 or (703) 683-8100; www.store.astd.org.

Orders for college text/course adoption use. Please contact Berrett-Koehler: Tel: (800) 929-2929; Fax: (802) 864-7626.

Orders by U.S. trade bookstores and wholesalers. Please contact Ingram Publisher Services, Tel: (800) 509-4887; Fax: (800) 838-1149; E-mail: customer.service@ingrampublisherservices.com; or visit www.ingrampublisherservices.com/Ordering for details about electronic publishing.

Library of Congress Cataloging-in-Publication Data

Bingham, Tony.
  The new social learning : a guide to transforming organizations through social media / by Tony Bingham and Marcia Conner.
    p. cm.
  Includes bibliographical references and index.
  ISBN 978-1-60509-702-2 (pbk. : alk. paper)
  1.   Social learning. 2.   Digital media--Social aspects. 3.   Online social networks. 4. Organizational change. I. Conner, Marcia, 1965- II. Title.

HQ784.M3B56 2010
303.3'2--dc22

                    2010026010

Copyediting: Tora Estep; Proofreading and indexing: Abella Publishing Services, LLC; Design and production: PerfecType, Nashville, TN; Cover art and design: Steve Fife

Contents

Foreword

♦ ♦ ♦

One afternoon in the early 1990s, I found myself at a meeting in my boss's cavernous office when one of the organization's computer support guys showed up to demonstrate a new-fangled technology called instant messaging. I'd never seen IM before, but I was intrigued—so I volunteered for the demo.

My boss settled in front of his computer. I stationed myself at another computer just outside the office. And away we went—typing and tapping a silent conversation in real time.

"Wow," I shouted to the others back in the room. "Very cool." And when I returned to the meeting, I offered—unsolicited, of course—my thoughts on what we'd just witnessed.

"This could be big," I said. "Instant messaging is going to be incredibly useful for the deaf and hearing impaired, who can't just pick up the phone and talk to someone. It's not something most people will use much, but for that slice of the population it's amazing."

Today, nearly two decades after instant messaging has become a part of everyday communication around the world—when literally tens of millions of people with perfectly good hearing are IM-ing right now—there's a moral to this tale: Sometimes we miss the point.

That's especially true of technology. In business terms, most people—myself included—think of Twitter, Facebook, and other social media as tools for *marketing*. But now that I've read this smart and incisive book, I realize that I might be as wrong about that as I was about that other young technology back in the early 1990s.

As Tony Bingham and Marcia Conner show in the pages that follow, the deepest, most enduring impact of social media might be on *learning*.

There's a certain intuitive, forehead-slapping logic to that insight. Of course! In so many ways, learning is a fundamentally social act. From circle time in kindergarten, to study groups in college, to team projects in the workforce, sociability has always greased the gears of learning.

But now wikis, multiplayer games, and social networking have taken that truth and vaulted it to new heights. "Our inherent drive to learn together can be facilitated through emerging technologies that extend, widen, and deepen our reach," Bingham and Conner write. These innovations, they argue, "enable a new kind of knowledge-building ecosystem with people at its core."

The New Social Learning is a terrific guide to that emerging ecosystem. It will give you a set of core principles—"playground rules," as the authors call them—to help you navigate it. And with examples that range from Best Buy to Intel and from Deloitte to the U.S. Central Intelligence Agency, it will show you how social media can improve the way you recruit talent, engage employees, and build a workforce's capacities.

Social learning isn't a replacement for training and employee development. But it can accomplish what traditional approaches often cannot. For instance, this new, technology-enabled approach can supplement instruction with collaboration and co-creation and, in so doing, blur the boundary between the instructor and the instructed and enhance the experience of all. It can leave a "digital audit trail" that reveals the path of a learning journey and allows others to retrace it. It can re-energize your conferences and retreats by providing a backchannel of feedback and questions. It can bring far-flung employees together into new communities in which they can not only learn from one another, but also fashion new offerings for customers. In short, social media can change the way your company works. As the authors put it, "Once you move away from the push of information to the pull of learning, you liberate creative powers in your people."

It's exciting when two of the most respected names in training and development come together to produce a work like *The New Social Learning*. When you read this book, you'll learn something—and, I'm convinced, you'll share its many insights.

But what you might share most of all is that Twitter, Facebook, and their social media kin aren't all about marketing. They're equally, if not more so, about learning. This book helped me understand that and avoid missing the point of a new technology once again. It can do the same for you.

Daniel H. Pink
Washington, D.C.
June 2010

Introduction

◆ ◆ ◆

Beyond the hype, buzzwords, and entertainment value of reconnecting with old friends, people in organizations across the globe use social media to collaborate and learn. Emerging technologies enable a new kind of knowledge-building ecosystem with people at its core.

Classic business models presume that relevant information is created and shared either through management or training. But classic isn't enough: There's too much to know and make sense of, too little time to gain perspective, and information changes too fast to dispense. A virtual water cooler becomes a gathering place to share ideas and ask questions beyond the limits of formal organizations, company meetings, or classrooms.

Our inherent drive to learn together can be facilitated through emerging technologies that extend, widen, and deepen our reach. More so than any other technology, social media allows us to embrace the needs of changing workplace demographics and enables people of all ages to learn in ways that are comfortable and convenient for them.

Today, networks of knowledgeable people, working across time and space, can make informed decisions and solve complex problems in ways they couldn't dream of years ago. By bringing together people who share interests, no matter their location or time zone, social media has the potential to transform the workplace into an environment where learning is as natural as it is powerful.

Although most writing about social media focuses on how to use it for marketing, we believe there's a larger story to tell. This book is for people who are specifically interested in how social media helps people in organizations learn quickly; innovate fast; share knowledge; and engage with peers, business partners, and the customers they serve.

We came together to write this book because the topic matters deeply to both of us even though we come to the subject from unique vantage points.

Tony leads a large professional association whose members help organizations achieve sustainable competitive advantage by building the knowledge and skills of their people. He is committed to helping executives and the training and development community align learning with the strategic priorities of the organization and to ensure they have the tools to build the capability of the workforce to achieve growth and success. And, as a result of years spent working in the technology sector, he has a personal passion for the power that collaborative tools have to create big change.

Marcia is a partner at a fast-moving firm that provides thought leadership, research, education, and advice on leveraging emerging digital strategies. She refines product strategies and market positions, while facilitating a cultural shift to prepare organizations to adopt social media, removing barriers in their path to success. With a long history in the workplace-learning field, often inside large enterprises, she brings a collaborative perspective to industries that seek to do more than just inform.

We wrote this book for senior executives, managers at all levels, and the people rising quickly to those posts. Rather than simply address leaders focused on education delivery models, trainers thinking about instructional design, or even technologists fascinated by tools, we explore the application of social media in all aspects of talent management: recruitment, engagement, retention, capacity, and capability. We look at the power of social learning and share compelling stories from companies that validate the value of collaborative technologies to elevate and accelerate business and employee impact.

The opening chapter addresses the trends reshaping the workplace, the challenges and opportunities these shifts create, and how the new social learning provides the flexibility and perspective required in times of change.

Each subsequent chapter focuses on one social media category and its application. Every chapter also tackles the business challenges these emerging practices can overcome and how to address critics as you wade into the social stream, providing recommendations on how you and your organization can begin to put these approaches to work. While we address technology, we recognize that the specific tools in use today may have changed dramatically by the time you read this book, so we've created a complementary website—http://thenewsociallearning.com—where you can learn more about the applications you may want to try. On that site, we also offer step-by-step "getting started" guides because readers will come to the topic with varying interest and levels of knowledge.

Although each chapter builds on the one before it, beginning with the broadest approaches and then narrowing in on more specific methods, we encourage you to read the first chapter and then skip to any other chapter that intrigues you, weaving your way back.

It is our hope that with a broad view of social media's power to transform your organization, you will garner wide participation and facilitate meaningful conversations, finding yourself ready to move forward with deeper understanding, concrete examples of success, and a renewed energy to learn.

Tony Bingham   Marcia Conner
@tonybingham   @marciamarcia
Alexandria, VA   Staunton, VA

Acknowledgments

◆ ◆ ◆

We wrote this book to help senior executives and managers understand the power of social media for learning. While developing this content, we used a variety of social tools to reach out to individuals and organizations for their insights and stories. We deeply appreciate the contributions of Kevin Renner at Chevron; Geoff Fowler, Don Burke, and Sean Dennehy at the CIA; Patricia Romeo at Deloitte; Jamie Pappas at EMC; Graham Brown-Martin at Learning Without Frontiers; Monty Flinsch at Mayo Clinic; Dan Pontefract at TELUS; and the more than 80 organizations and thought leaders who shared their expertise with us so that we could share it with you. By describing their challenges and successes, the examples included in this book demonstrate the tremendous impact social media can have in companies and for communities, and for those who engage with them. We hope their examples inspire you as much as they have inspired us.

In addition, John Seely Brown, Howard Rheingold, Nancy White, Judee Humberg, Stowe Boyd, Andrea Baker, Etienne Wenger, and Andy McAfee continued to illuminate our path. Doug Newburg, Steve LeBlanc, and Wayne Hodgins ensured overarching themes rang true in the heart as well as the intellect. Practitioners who graciously furthered this topic included Jane Bozarth, Aaron Silvers, Koreen Olbrish, Paula Thornton, Luis Suarez, Ellen Wagner, Stan Garfield, Luis Benitez, Mark Oehlert, Jane Hart, and Jay Cross.

Marcia also wants to thank Jennifer, Anya, Karey, Connie, April, Christine, Valerie, and Lisa, who provided encouragement and support to create the space for writing while their children reminded her that socialness is not secondary to or separate from learning. Laura Fitton and Linda Ziffrin created an oasis filled with tender care and humor. Her husband, Karl, provided compassion, patience, and understanding in a way that proved diplomacy can exist amid last-minute meals, late-night conversations, and laptop-laden vacations.

The teams at ASTD and Berrett-Koehler exemplified a true partnership. Jennifer Homer, specifically, was herculean as she lifted our loads, managing the process, organizing the troops, and offering kind words at precisely the right time. Pat Galagan turned big ideas into consumable passages, and Tora Estep smoothed out our words.

For this particular journey we want to thank more than the people we interacted with directly. We also owe thanks to those who envisioned and developed the social tools that augmented our work. This process hummed along with the aide of MacBooks, ThinkPads, iPads, iPhones, Twitter, Facebook, Google Docs, MindManager, Socialcast, and Socialtext.

Together this extraordinary team made quick work of a daunting task, and we will be appreciative forever.

The NEW Social Learning
Playground Rules

1. No loitering in the playground areas. The value is in participation and engagement.

2. The playground is for people of all ages.

3. Only people interested in having influence are allowed on the premises.

4. Abusive, spammy, or intolerant behavior is not tolerated. Sarcasm, debate, and challenging and calling out bull are welcome, though.

5. If you feed pigeons, be warned they may poop on you.

6. Keep excessive cussing, name calling, and partisan politics away from the pool.

7. Enjoy life offline to stay interesting online.

8. The right to be heard does not include the right to be taken seriously.

9. Be patient, above all, with yourself.

Failure to obey these rules can result in missing an unprecedented opportunity to learn with smart, interesting people across the globe.

The 36,000-Foot View

When I look back over the past few years, I see the evolution and the growth of a program, of an organization, and of a community. I see learning. I see dynamic interaction among experts in social and online media and those involved in the creation and conveyance of intelligence. It's time to expand that conversation, to talk about innovation beyond tools—to talk about innovation as an art, as a behavior, and as a necessity for survival and progress. Growth and adaptation are part of a journey, one that cannot be successful if taken alone. And so we come together.

—Geoffrey Fowler

Editor-in-Chief, The CIA World Intelligence Review *(WIRe)*

◆ ◆ ◆

"Load the boat."

The phrase played over and over in his head while he boarded the plane.

As he took his seat, uncertainty ate at him, distracted him, turning the plane's cabin into one large noise. He was tired but had work to do. A couple chatted continuously in the seats behind him. It would be a long flight.

He unpacked his carryon, then let his head fall back, eyes closed. The meeting had been tough. He knew what he had to do to rebuild the business and with it his job. And he had to begin before tomorrow morning's meeting. In his mind, he started loading the boat.

He'd first heard the phrase at the university hospital where his wife had been cared for, and he'd asked a resident what it meant. "It means you're not alone. If you have a problem, if you need help, if you need to learn something new, there's a team of people you can call on at any time." Over the course of his wife's treatment, he'd watched the medical team use every means they had to stay in touch with people they trusted, the team they'd built. These people learned in real time in real-life situations. They saved lives; they had saved her life. Maybe their approach to collaboration could save his business, too.

He had all the tools. He had his team. He'd done the work. He was well informed, but something was still missing.

When he started to load the boat in his mind, the noise of the plane disappeared. His fear and uncertainty dissipated. As the plane settled in, the Dave Matthews Band played through the earbuds his daughter had given him before the flight. He read email and watched a short video clip. Then he used the plane's wireless connection to check email and scan his social net. What he had to do turned into what he wanted to do. He had found his rhythm.

The computer screen danced in front of him. His fingers became an extension of his mind. His smartphone and laptop worked together as his fingers flew. What felt heavy before seemed weightless at 36,000 feet.

Tweets and texts flooded in from his worldwide team about the board members' perspectives, making it clear where his energy needed to take him. He filled in the missing piece of the presentation. He shared with his team, and he found his voice. He knew he'd succeed.

Load the boat. Instantly recall what you've been trained to do and put it to work. Learn as you do. Engage instead of escape. Thrive instead of survive. This is social learning at its best. Noise turned into music. Colleagues turned into collaborators. A symphony. The next day a board member said it best: "Pure music."

The Workplace Has Changed

At this moment, your people are already learning with social media. They have already begun to reach out and connect in new and powerful ways. The question is, will you come along? Do you want to play a part in what and how they learn? Or do you want to try to stop them? Will you restrict them or free them to do the work you hired them to do? The work you do *with* them?

Workplace learning is a competitive advantage for every company. People need to learn fast, as part of the ebb and flow of their jobs, not just on the rare occasion they are in a class. Senior leaders urgently want to provide their people with something vibrant, effective, and cutting-edge to support their nonstop learning—something that will ensure that competitive edge.

As organizations search for ways to increase profits, save money, and compete, lighter and friendlier tools have become available to help them excel. These social media tools are changing the way people work, usually bypassing formal training altogether.

Fundamentally, this book is about how people learn socially, often but not always with technology. This book is not a plea to reorganize the training department or turn it into the social media team, although some of you may decide to do that. We will show how people in organizations can work together more effectively across departments with their employees, partners, and customers, aided by social media in the stream of work. We will show how this approach imbues learning into the essence of work and how it makes learning a valuable, ongoing process.

We don't focus on the tools here. They change fast, and we have set up a website where the details about the technologies can stay fresh. Visit the site at http://thenewsociallearning.com. There you can contribute to the conversation and locate up-to-date information.

We encourage you to use this book to discover how social media tools facilitate learning, how they might be leveraged to extend and expand your interactions with colleagues, and how to use them to create something vibrant. As Chris Brogan, one of the top bloggers in the world, coauthor of *Trust Agents*, and author of *Social Media 101* says, "Focus on connecting with the people, and the tools will all make sense."[1]

Social learning is a fundamental shift in how people work—leveraging how we have always worked, but now with new tools to accelerate and broaden individual and organizational reach.

What Is the New Social Learning?

To understand social learning, we must first understand social media. Social media is a set of Internet-based technologies designed to be used by three or more people. It's rarer than it sounds. Most interaction supported by technology is narrowcast (one to one), often with a telephone call or an email message; niche-cast (one to small groups), for instance using email distribution lists or small-circulation newsletters; or broadcast (one to many), as in large-scale online magazines or a radio show.

Social learning is what it sounds like—learning with and from others. It has been around for a long time and naturally occurs at conferences, in groups, and among old friends in a café as easily as it does in classroom exercises or among colleagues online who have never met in person. We experience it when we go down the hall to ask a question and when we post that same question on Twitter anticipating that someone will respond.

While social media is technology used to engage three or more people and social learning is participating with others to make sense of new ideas, what's new is how powerfully they work together. Social tools leave a digital audit trail, documenting our learning journey—often an unfolding story—and leaving a path for others to follow.

Tools are now available to facilitate social learning that is unconstrained by geographic differences (spatial boundaries) or time-zone differences (temporal boundaries) among team members.

The new social learning reframes social media from a marketing strategy to a strategy that encourages knowledge transfer and connects people in a way consistent with how we naturally interact. It is not a delivery system analogous to classroom training, mobile learning, or e-learning. Instead it's a powerful approach to sharing and discovering a whole array of options—some of which we may not even know we need—leading to more informed decision making and a more intimate, expansive, and dynamic understanding of the culture and context in which we work.

The new social learning provides people at every level, in every nook of the organization, and every corner of the globe, a way to reclaim their natural capacity to learn non-stop. Social learning can help the pilot fly more safely, the saleswoman be more persuasive, and the doctor keep up to date.

For a long time, many of us have known learning could transform the workplace. We longed for tools to catch up with that potential. Only recently have changes in corporate culture and technology allowed this eventuality to unfold.

Clay Shirky, who writes about web economics and teaches new media at New York University and author of *Cognitive Surplus*, points out, "Prior to the Internet, the last technology that had any real effect on the way people sat down and talked together was the table."[2]

At its most basic level, new social learning can result in people becoming more informed, gaining a wider perspective, and being able to make better decisions by engaging with others. It acknowledges that learning happens with and through other people, as a matter of participating in a community, not just by acquiring knowledge.

> *Prior to the Internet, the last technology that had any real effect on the way people sat down and talked together was the table.*

Social learning happens using social media tools and through extended access and conversations with all our connections—in our workplaces, our communities, and online. It happens when we keep the conversation going on a blog rich with comments, through coaching and mentoring, or even during a workout at the gym.

Social learning is augmented by commercial tools, such as Facebook, Twitter, YouTube, blogs, and wikis, and with enterprise applications and suites of applications including Socialtext, Socialcast, Newsgator, and Lotus Connections. With some custom development, learning also can grow on enterprise social platforms such as IBM WebSphere Portal Server, Microsoft Sharepoint, SAP Netweaver Portal and Collaboration, and Oracle's Beehive.

Don't conclude this is all new, though. Social software has been around for almost 50 years, dating back to the Plato bulletin board system. Networks such as Compuserve, Usenet, discussion boards, and The Well were around before the founder of Facebook was even born. Only technology enthusiasts used those systems, though, because of clunky interfaces that didn't readily surface or socialize the best ideas.

The new social learning is enabled by easy-to-use, socially focused, and commercially available "Web 2.0" tools and "Enterprise 2.0" software that move services, assets, smarts, and guidance closer to where they are needed—to people seeking answers, solving problems, overcoming uncertainty, and improving how they work. They facilitate collaboration and inform choices on a wide stage, fostering learning from a vast, intellectually diverse set of people.

> *Training often gives people solutions to problems already solved. Collaboration addresses challenges no one has overcome before.*

These new social tools augment training, knowledge management, and communications practices used today. They can introduce new variables that can fundamentally change getting up to speed, provide a venue to share spontaneously developed resources as easily as finely polished documents, and draw in departments that previously hadn't considered themselves responsible for employee development at all.

Social tools are powerful building blocks that can transform the way we enable learning and development in organizations. They foster a new culture of sharing, one in which content is contributed and distributed with few restrictions or costs.

Most of what we learn at work and elsewhere comes from engaging in networks where people co-create, collaborate, and share knowledge, fully participating and actively engaging, driving, and guiding their learning through whatever topics will help them improve. Training often gives people solutions to problems already solved. Collaboration addresses challenges no one has overcome before.

The new social learning makes that immediate, enabling people to easily interact with those with whom they share a workplace, a passion, a curiosity, a skill, or a need.

The new social learning allows us, as Stowe Boyd who first coined the term *social tools* and has been working for two decades observing how they affect business, media, and society puts it, "[to grow] bigger than my

What It's Not

Another way to think about the new social learning is to compare it with what it is not.

- ◆ **The new social learning is not just for knowledge workers.** It can empower people who work on shop floors, backstage, on the phone, behind retail counters, and on the battlefield. It is not your corporate intranet, although features of social learning may be included there. Document management, calendaring, blogs, and online directories may contribute to learning socially, but they are often task oriented rather than community oriented.

- ◆ **It's not at odds with formal education**. Students often use Twitter as a back channel for communicating among themselves or with instructors. Teachers can also use social media before and after classes to capture and share everyone's ideas.

- ◆ **It's not a replacement for training or employee development.** Training is well suited for compliance, deep learning, and credentialing. Formal development programs are still needed to prepare employees to progress through the organization. Social learning can supplement training and development in the classroom or online. It complements training and covers knowledge that formal training is rarely able to provide.

- ◆ **It's not synonymous with informal learning,** a term often used to describe anything that's not learned in a formal program or class. The broad category of informal learning can include social learning, but some instances of informal learning are not social—for example, search and reading.

- ◆ **It's not a new interface for online search,** which could only be considered social because other people developed the content you discover. Finding content with a search engine does not involve interpersonal engagement—a hallmark of social learning.

- ◆ **It's not the same as e-learning,** the term used to describe any use of technology to teach something intentionally. That broad category can include social tools and, if it's organized using an online learning community such as Moodle, can be quite communal.

- ◆ **It's not constantly social in the same way a party is.** Often people are alone when they are engaged and learning through social tools. The socialness refers to the way interaction happens: intermingling ideas, information, and experiences, resulting in something more potent than any individual contribution.

head. I want to create an idea space where I can think outside my mind, leveraging my connections with others."[3]

Moving Theory Into Practice

A "social learning theory" was first put forward in 1954, standing on the shoulders of John Dewey and drawing on the budding fields of sociology, behavior modification, and psychology applied to understanding and changing conduct.[4] Ideas from social learning theory informed the thinking of later learning theorists, including Albert Bandura who wrote in 1977, "Learning would be exceedingly laborious, not to mention hazardous, if people had to rely solely on the effects of their own actions to inform them what to do. Fortunately, most human behavior is learned observationally through modeling."[5]

The early focus of social learning theory was learning socially appropriate behavior by imitating others, which is only a small aspect of how social learning is used in practice today. Given the recent explosion of means for people to learn socially and the vast array of topics that can be learned from others, it's unfortunate what was called social learning had such a limited scope. Recognizing this, there will be times we shorten "the new social learning" to "social learning" here and in our work elsewhere to describe the broader issues and opportunity now available. Social learning is modeling, observation, and so much more.

Social constructivism is the theory of knowledge that seems to best describe how people learn together, whether in person or online. When you engage with people, you build your own insight into what's being discussed. Someone else's understanding complements yours, and together you start to weave an informed interpretation. You tinker until you can move on.

Swiss psychologist Jean Piaget laid the groundwork for this approach by challenging the behaviorist notion popular in the 1950s that people were passive recipients of external stimuli that shaped how they behaved.[6] Instead, Piaget conducted many experiments to demonstrate that people are active participants in their learning. They interpret what's around them based on their unique current understanding of the world, and then they continually modify their understanding as they encounter new information. Piaget's discoveries eventually led to the concept and practice of discovery learning for children and the use of role-play and simulation for adults. Active participation is the key in both cases.

This set the stage for Peter Berger's and Thomas Luckman's *social construction of reality*, which led to the prominence of social constructivism.[7] We are social creatures. If we play an active role in creating our views of reality, then the groups we participate in also contribute. Our reality is shaped by our social interactions. These exchanges provide context—socially scaffolding what you have already learned with what another person has learned and so on. This generates a virtuous spiral, socially generated and built and more powerful than any one participant could create individually.

In a world of rapid change, we each need to garner as much useful information as possible, sort through it in a way that meets our unique circumstances, calibrate it with what we already know, and re-circulate it with others who share our goals.

The new social learning leverages online communities, media sharing, microsharing, content collaboration, and immersive environments to introduce people to ideas in quick bursts, when it suits their workflow, without a big learning curve, and in a way that more closely mirrors how groups interact in person.

Social constructivism has become timely because work has for so long focused on what's known. To triumph today, we must now understand new information and complex concepts—what hasn't been known before and is often more complicated than one person can figure out alone.

The 21st century mind is a collective mind where we access what we know in our friends' and colleagues' brains. Together we can be smarter and can address ever more challenging problems. What we store in our heads may not be as important as all that we can tap in our networks. Together we are better.

Why Is This Happening Now?

The convergence of three key trends accelerates the need for social learning. Although some of these trends have been observable for decades, their influence compounds.

Three Converging Workforce Trends
- ♦ Expanding opportunities for personal connection
- ♦ Emerging expectations from shifting workforce demographics
- ♦ Increasing reach of customized technology

Expanding Opportunities for Personal Connection

We have always been social creatures. We have been naturally driven to communicate, converse, and share with one another since our ancestors came into being. This is part of our survival mechanism as well as our natural preference. Our ability to converse and share with one another has always been expanding.

When people on the farm worked with their neighbors, putting up a barn or exchanging wheat for corn, they shared information about a harvesting technique or a new recipe. They created and sustained social capital—the stock of social trust, norms, and networks developed through a flow of information and reciprocity drawn upon to solve common problems. Social capital became financial capital as two farmers who exchanged tools could do more while buying less.

The opportunities ramped up as transportation enabled us to become more mobile and expanded the number of people we could socialize with around town. Then the phone let our voices do the travelling and negated the requirement for us to be in the same place as those we wanted to talk with. As telephone lines expanded globally, distance became even less of a barrier for conversation and connections. As satellites and cellular and computer networks came online, we became able to communicate with anyone and everyone, anywhere and anytime.

Communication and collaboration reached a tipping point with email and online forums, then instant messaging, then voice over Internet, then video. Just as we thought we couldn't possibly be any more connected, our social nature fueled yet another expansion as we formed alliances and human networks of distributed organizations using commercially available then inside-the-firewall media tools.

These connections represent more than an expanding volume of conversations. We are witnessing a dramatic increase in our collective thinking, collaboration, and capacity to grow. Doug Engelbart, the father of personal computing, was prescient when he pondered a collective IQ half a century ago:

> What if, suddenly, in an evolutionary sense, we evolved a super new nervous system to upgrade our collective social organisms? [What if] we got strategic and began to form cooperative alliances, employing advanced networked computer tools and methods to develop and apply new collective knowledge?[8]

We may now be realizing this dream. An opportunity to raise personal, organizational, and collective IQ has arrived. As stressed as our communication capabilities seem today, history shows this trend will continue as we figure out how to more effectively connect, collaborate, converse, and learn. We need to embrace the opportunity for personal connections and be willing to evolve.

Emerging Expectations from Shifting Workplace Demographics

Think back to the year you joined the workforce. Then reflect on how things were about six months into that job. Did you think you should be given the opportunity to make big splashes and reap rich rewards? Did you consider your off hours your own, reserved to pursue your passions? Many of us did. Yet we forget that when we label newcomers to the workforce as unrealistic about advancement or uninterested in working hard.

Some of the qualities associated with the youngest generations in the workforce today are qualities of age, not generation. Brashness, dissatisfaction with the status quo, and constant questioning are characteristics many of us had when we were young. Because we didn't have Facebook connections with friends reinforcing our perspectives, let alone magazines and blogs showcasing young people who became chief executive officers at 19, we abandoned those mindsets to fit in.

Have your expectations of the workplace changed in this newly connected world? Are many things the same as they were as recently as last year? If you were to go to work for your company now, would you not have higher expectations than you had in the past? We certainly would.

Our wide look at demographic shifts has convinced us that organizations of all types and sizes have a lot to learn and do differently if they are to attract and keep the talent—of all ages—they need to succeed. It's not all about Millennials (also known as the Net Generation and Generation Y). Many of us, their older colleagues, also find that new social technologies allow us to work in ways we never believed would happen in our lifetime.

These shifts are about everyone in the workforce. We don't discount the generational factor; we simply see it as part of the whole.

We believe differences in generation, gender, and consumer outlook together provide a useful framework to address a changing workforce and workplace. Success will go to those businesses savvy enough to understand, learn from, and leverage these shifts.

We should aspire to create a workplace that uses the talents of everyone, connecting them in meaningful ways, regardless of differences in generation, gender, and consumer outlook.

Generation

By 2014, potentially half the workforce will be from Millennials. Overall, this generation has a high comfort level with technology and broad expectations about using it to learn. The previous generation, Generation X, shares many of these expectations but has learned to navigate slow-to-change workplaces. Millennials and generations after are not as apt to put up with inefficient ways.

Fairly soon, Generation Z will begin entering the workforce. They are even more intimate with technology and have higher expectations for instant answers and constant connectivity than Millennials.

Baby Boomers have already begun to retire. Although the perception exists that older workers do not widely embrace technology, a recent survey by ASTD shows that 79 percent of Baby Boomers, compared with 76 percent of Millennials, believe that social media tools are not being used enough for education activities within organizations.[9]

Generations

Depending on the author or commentator, the dates that demarcate the generations can vary. For the purposes of this book, we've used the Pew Research Center's report titled "Millennials: A Portrait of Generation Next."

- ◆ Baby Boomers: 1946–1964
- ◆ Generation X: 1965–1980
- ◆ Millennials, Net Generation, or Gen Y: 1981–1997
- ◆ Generation Z: After 1997.

Source: Pew Research Center, Millennials: A Portrait of Generation Next (Washington, D.C.: Pew Research Center, 2010).

Gender

To add to the demographic shift, estimates suggest that within this decade nearly 60 percent of the workforce will be female, a group more likely to turn to its social networks for insights and perspectives than males.[10] Studies show that women experience a physiological and emotional change when they connect verbally—and combined with new ways to easily maintain, organize, and create new connections, these networks demonstrate value to women more quickly because these connections feel more like experiences they have off line.

Consumer Outlook

Another shifting workplace influence is consumer savvy. Rich media around us everywhere—on TV, on the Internet, in stores, and on mobile

---

Personal Matters

Regardless of generation or gender, most employees no longer have someone staying at home to handle personal matters while they are at work. To take care of ourselves, we divide our energy and focus between work and home. Organizations that prohibit this through policy or technology controls become poor guardians of their employees and limit their capacity to attend to small items that may become big distractions.

When people of all ages rely on technology, they see they can work anytime, anyplace, and that they should be evaluated on work results—not on how, when, or where it was done.

---

phones—have changed our expectations about communication inside our companies, too. We bring our knowledge and assumptions from the marketplace to work. As a result, we are no longer willing to put up with hard-to-manage interfaces, poor quality events, or questionably useful design because we now know—we've experienced—better alternatives.

Increasing Reach of Customized Technology

As consumers, we have grown to expect manufacturers and retailers to customize all sorts of things for us: houses, personal computers, jeans, sneakers, credit card billing cycles, and so on. A new breed of technology and new forms of distribution replace a long history of mass production with mass customization.

This trend is moving to the workplace in *mashups*, assembling unique items to create something new. Producing new results from pre-existing bits and pieces can result in new songs, new software, new courses, and new job roles.

Wayne Hodgins, a futurist focused on technology, standards, and knowledge creation, coined the term "snowflake effect" to describe the exponentially growing trend toward extreme mass customization for every person, every day.[11]

We see four types of mashups influencing how people learn socially: role, workgroup, content, and management.

Role Mashups

Although the word mashup is new, in the 1970s, Alvin Toffler wrote that a society neatly divided into producers and consumers would change to one composed of "prosumers" who would produce and consume.[12]

A similar blurring of roles occurs in social learning with everyone acting as both learners and teachers. Rather than simply doing two jobs, the mashing up of roles creates a whole new way of working.

This intersection can be credited with the rapid adoption of social media in society. It fundamentally changes our level of participation from being recipients to being creators and innovators, heightening engagement and focus in the same way that knowing we are going to write about or teach something heightens our senses as we take in new information.

Mashups change work's traditional linear and separate roles into a culture of co-production, co-design, and co-development, mixing responsibilities among everyone involved in a new cyclical process. In the case of the new social learning, it's not about simply giving people online communities or wikis and getting out of the way. It is about a new iterative and inclusive model where anyone is able to create, use, publish, remix, repurpose, and learn.

Workgroup Mashups

Global connections are creating what *New York Times* columnist Thomas L. Friedman calls a "flat world," where we can reach, team up with, and learn from people everywhere.[13] Through collaboration, outside the boundaries of traditional hierarchies and located anywhere on the planet, people can join forces to produce content, goods, and services.

In writing this book, we were able to assemble instant workgroups of people by sending queries over Twitter, engaging with those who follow us online, running ideas and questions by them, seeking their opinions and data they might know of to back up our hunches, and asking about the objections and arguments they hear and how they overcome them. Through these means we found relevant articles, organizations with compelling stories, critics to consult, and supporters who extended what we thought about these topics in ways that strengthened what we wanted to say.

Content Mashups

With the Internet, anyone can find almost anything about a topic. Often, we don't need to create new content because all the parts we need already exist. Mashups allow us to quickly access these relevant bits of existing information and put them together to form a new combination just right for the current need.

Sites such as Slideshare let you see collections of slides and enable downloading so you can pick out individual slides and mix and modify them to create your own just-right slide set. Slideshare also enables people to share comments, identify favorites, make recommendations, and find other content you might also like.

Thumbs-up and thumbs-down ratings on websites such as Reddit collectively create new content. When you add comments or assign stars evaluating your experiences with a product, service, or site, you also create new content.

Add to that fresh insights, some riffed on by others, when we share this information over Twitter, Facebook, or an in-house equivalent, or when we create a social bookmark using Digg or Delicious, where we add our perspectives and opinions on existing bits of content such as web pages, blogs, and articles.

Management Mashups

Leaders have always conveyed their visions. Now they use blogs, email, newsletters, video, and audio to widen their reach and to engage co-workers in a conversation.

The head of Intel's human resources learning and development group took this further by posting his semi-annual assessment scores to the entire Intel learning and development community and inviting discussion on a global level. In effect, he used a mashup to say, "Let's talk. How can I work on these things?" He used the technology Intel uses for collaboration (a companywide wiki) and feedback about him personally (his review) in a forum where people could add their perspectives on him and the organization to create something that hadn't existed before. He also asked people to be his employees and customers, coaches, and teachers. His role modeling and risk taking led to further conversations about being more strategic as a group and sped up how everyone learns.

Bob Picciano, general manager of IBM software sales, uses social tools inside IBM to reach out to his immediate teams and quicken the pace for people to reach corporate executives. He makes traditional hierarchies more blurred and more dynamic, getting the job done through networks and communities. When asked by Luis Suarez, social computing evangelist at IBM, how it feels for a very busy leader to use social tools while at work, Picciano responded, "Liberating! It's liberating to let command and control go."[14]

"In many cases you aren't giving up control—you are shifting it to someone else that you have confidence in," says Charlene Li, founder of Altimeter Group and author of *Groundswell* and *Open Leadership*. "More than anything else, the past few years have been dominated by the rise of a *culture of sharing*. This new culture has created an additional, timelier way to listen and, more importantly, opens it up to anyone in the organization who is willing to learn."[15]

> *These new social tools can enable organizations to strike a balance between surfacing the knowledge people need and giving them the ease and freedom to learn in a healthy and open way.*

Because of technological advances, especially social tools, we are no longer just surfing the Internet: In some ways, we are becoming the Internet. We are no longer following leaders: We are leading and influencing people and organizations. The Internet is becoming our supporting infrastructure. The power of mashups, the power of social media itself, is the inclusion, interoperability, sharing, and iteration that are so very human and social.

Learning can easily occur anytime, anywhere, and in a variety of formats. It always has, but now it's codified and easy for others to see. These new social tools can enable organizations to strike a balance between surfacing the knowledge people need and giving them the ease and freedom to learn in a healthy and open way.

Is This Learning?

Often when we talk about these trends and technologies, people ask us how we define *learning*.

We define learning as the transformative process of taking in information that, when internalized and mixed with what we have experienced, changes what we know and builds on what we can do. It's based on input, process, and reflection. It is what changes us.

By pigeonholing a very small segment of this transformative process with labels such as *formal* and *informal*, we marginalize learning. And so the rich and exciting conversations that transform people stop being considered learning at all. They get called communications, marketing, pre-sales, or customer support.

Learning is what makes us more vibrant participants in a world seeking fresh perspectives, novel insights, and first-hand experiences. When shared, what we have learned mixes with what others have learned, then ripples out, transforming organizations, enterprises, ecosystems, and the society around us.

Training, knowledge management, good leadership, and a whole host of organizational practices can add to an environment where people learn, but people can learn without this assistance, too.

In what is known as the 70/20/10 learning concept, Robert Eichinger and Michael Lombardo, in collaboration with Morgan McCall of the Center for Creative Leadership, explain that 70 percent of learning and development takes place from real-life and on-the-job experiences, tasks, and problem solving; 20 percent of the time development comes from other people through informal or formal feedback, mentoring, or coaching; and 10 percent of learning and development comes from formal training.[16]

To help see learning in a broader way, think of five people you communicate with and then identify at least three things you learned from each. Most people find this easier than recalling information they learned in a formal setting—not because they weren't offered useful topics to learn—but because when we connect with people, the exchange sticks with us. That engagement calls up something from within us or connects with an emotion, and that mental dance leaves a footprint we can walk in again. Reflecting on it later improves learning even more.

Some formal training programs are designed for gaining new skills or competencies. A new emergency medical technician (EMT) may not remember all the steps for cardiopulmonary resuscitation (CPR), but when she needs to use it, her body knows what to do. That learning is about more than recall, too. It's also about building muscle memory and a warehouse of options when the need to resuscitate someone arises.

Other training programs are for expanding your thinking or capacity to deal with situations ahead. The same is true of learning with people. This also comes from the community around you, in person or online. Etienne Wenger, author of *Digital Habitats, Communities of Practice, Situated Learning,* and other books, asserts that human knowing is fundamentally a social act.[17] By hearing about the experiences of others, you mash up snippets of data, add them to your own, and fit them into your sense of who you are and what you can do—together and with others. "To learn is to optimize the quality of one's networks," says Jay Cross, author of *Work Smarter* and *Informal Learning.* "Learning is social. Most learning is collaborative. Other people are providing the context and the need, even if they're not in the room."[18]

The traditional model of corporate training, where experts disseminate knowledge in one-time training events or someone presents all day, is being modernized. It needs to take full advantage of the larger opportunity for incidental learning, learning from interacting with others, and learning along the way in the course of work.

Organizations and individuals will not be sufficiently served only by formal training. Diverse backgrounds and learning styles, and especially the complexity of people's jobs, determine what and how they learn. More critically, much of what needs to be learned is moving faster than we can create structured learning opportunities. Traditional training methods may be useful for teaching highly specific tasks or safety procedures, but evolving practices require more. Ad hoc and self-directed learning becomes a key strategy when we need to move fast.

> *To learn is to optimize the quality of one's networks. Learning is social. Most learning is collaborative. Other people are providing the context and the need, even if they're not in the room.*

The new social learning, which centers on information sharing, collaboration, and co-creation—not instruction—implies that the notion of training needs to expand. Marc Rosenberg, author of *E-Learning* and

Beyond E-Learning, points out, "The metaphor of the classroom must make room for the metaphor of the library and the town hall."[19]

Studies show that we learn what we need to solve problems and inform decisions in the real world. Learning and work strategist Harold Jarche often says, "Work is learning, learning work."[20] Knowledge acquired but never put to use is usually forgotten. We may act as if we care about learning something and go through the motions, but we will forget it unless it is something we want to learn and it fits how we work.

Social learning is especially good at "loading the boat," showing us that for any crisis or just to satisfy our curiosity, there is a network to support us at any time. It's what Howard Rheingold, who teaches about "virtual community" (a term he coined) and social media at the University of California–Berkeley and at Stanford University and author of books including *The Virtual Community* and *SmartMobs,* describes as the "online brain trust representing a highly varied accumulation of expertise."[21]

Social learning is also very good at giving people a view into the little moments that happen between big activities, modeling behavior for others to observe, retain, and replicate—or avoid. We look across the tweet stream and tuck away lessons of finessed customer service calls, graceful endings to overlong presentations, and recoveries from cultural *faux pas* in front of visiting clients. Together we are better.

New developments such as life-like simulations, immersive environments, and ever more intelligent searches hold the promise of a new way—a deeper way—to connect and gain context-rich information that can transform us and thereby affect the organization, the society, and the people we serve.

How to Respond to Critics

One of the largest roadblocks to getting started on any new initiative is having the courage to face those who think what you're doing is dangerous or dumb. Maybe they have heard a story of someone doing something that scares them. Perhaps it's the unknown itself. Here are the most common stumbling blocks we hear about with regard to social learning and ways we believe you can address them. Each chapter provides a similar section to arm you with helpful ways to respond to critics.

Our Organization Will Never Embrace Social Media

The move to go social isn't a binary decision. Think of it as a Likert scale, where the truth is somewhere in the middle.

With no plans to use social media, organizations often ease into it. Microsharing works its way in because of an enterprise tool that can be implemented for free. Employees may be encouraged to comment on company blogs or to blog on their own. Perhaps an employee directory goes online and then someone creates a wiki. In some organizations, many adopt it, some even sponsor it, but it is not universally supported.

This is what embracing social media and the new social learning looks like. This is not jumping off the high dive. It's a process of adapting and adopting.

There are many ways to do this. Begin where you are and build where it suits your culture and environment. Just don't quash social media because you don't understand it. Learn from those who do.

People Will Say Inappropriate Things

If someone puts inappropriate content on the office door, you don't remove the door. If someone makes a tasteless joke over the telephone, you don't take away the phone. Social tools are often held to higher standards than traditional business tools because they are new, and bad stories circulate—go viral—quickly. Rather than ban the use of social tools, educate people how to use them effectively for work. They are the future of collaboration and learning at work, so the more you prepare people for how to use the tools respectfully and how to apply good social practices, the better. Also remember that people determined to harm you already have and always will find a way.

People Will Post Incorrect Information

One leader we spoke with expressed his concern this way, "Our employees may someday graffiti versions of our logo all over town, but we don't want to hand out spray paint." He feared that encouraging the use of social media tools would encourage his people to write posts he wouldn't approve of.

If anything, organizations have more stories about how the opposite is happening or at least how misnomers are cleaned up quickly. When questions and answers take place in public, a greater likelihood exists that someone will correct misrepresented facts, old data, and rumors or speculation and that people, realizing their responses will be widely seen, will work toward accuracy (or at least as they perceive it).

Details of wide-ranging accuracy spread non-stop among co-workers and the market you serve. Information about your organization seeps out when people talk in restaurants over lunch or speak on a mobile phone while waiting in line at the post office. When you provide venues where people can share peer to peer and be accountable, the best information rises to the top because many people have rated it as useful. Different voices can weigh in and correct stuff. It is the wisdom of crowds, to borrow the term made popular by James Surowiecki.[22]

Most organizations we spoke with while researching this book do lock down some data from their enterprise resource planning (ERP) systems, especially human resources details, so people cannot change data without appropriate approvals. Rather than aim for total control (which is elusive), expand your circle of trust.

Our People Need Training, Not Socializing

Learning socially does not replace training. It may overlap a little and complement a lot, but it can address the knowledge transfer that training may never get to.

Ellen Wagner, learning industry analyst for Sage Road Solutions, notes that "Today we assess personal mastery of knowledge and skills with how well people can leverage their interconnected networks of connections to resources, information, and subject matter specialists. Workplace success has shifted from individual accomplishment to teams, communities of practice, and collaboration."[23]

"The most significant thing going on in workplace training and development today is that we have punched through the walls of the classroom to allow experts and peers to bring their messages closer to work and life through technology," adds Allison Rossett, professor emerita of educational technology at San Diego State University. "I had my doubts about the 'learningfulness' of social nets until I began to use one as a key aspect of a graduate class on performance consulting. I don't anymore. My students worked in teams, conducted research, created presentations, sought experts, stirred up conversations—even conflict—and endeavored to engage people beyond our registered classmates. Maybe 65 students over two years have been real students in the class, but we have touched more than 500 as they join, use, and add to the online net. It was much better in almost every way."[24]

These Systems Compromise Classified Information

Organizations such as the U.S. Central Intelligence Agency (CIA), Wells Fargo, and the Mayo Clinic use social media widely even though their data are very sensitive. Rather than pronounce this new approach unfit for their environments, they practice good governance. They remind people to participate in online information-sharing communities with a full understanding that they bear responsibility for protecting sensitive or classified details.

"If you bring too many locks into an overly cautious culture, that's all you get: locks," says Chris Rasmussen, "living intelligence" and mashup evangelist within the U.S. intelligence community.[25]

This Can't Be Governed

Rather than start with a large, heavy-handed policy condemning the use of social media, put in place simple rules stating when people should use which tool to communicate, create, or share specific types of information. Make it easier for people to classify information they create. Specify which data and content are appropriate for what use—especially use within the company. Also, the fact that people can see what others share provides a reason to self-monitor and for people to monitor each other. See the appendix for examples of governance policies.

Although many enterprises today constrain employee access to social media on the Internet at work, there are few ways to block all social media use by employees unless you forbid them from using their personal smartphones entirely. Foster instead good practices and educated decision making for a longer-term solution.

This Can't Be Measured

Network-oriented web analytics can capture how these tools and our practices evolve. They are ideal for measuring four things:

- initiative (how many people logged in)
- persistence (how many people came back, presumably because they found value)
- connection (how the network expanded)
- technology transition (fewer documents sent across email).

The transparent nature of social media makes it easier to measure what's going on because it can be observed and tracked. For instance, you can analyze what people are searching for and map what they find. You can analyze not only where people go with their social tools, but also how they get there, how long they stay, and what they do when they are there. Although this does not verify the transfer of knowledge or skills, it is a pretty good indication.

Good measures look at functional outcomes rather than simply asking, "Did they learn?" There is little value to the organization if people don't apply what they take in. The best measures go the next step to connect using new skills and knowledge with how they affect measures such as the bottom line.

The Next Level

Senior leaders consider employees' knowledge a strategic priority, yet they often leave the topic of learning out of strategy discussions because years ago they relegated it to the training department. Over the past 15 years, companies have striven to transform organizational learning by streamlining the training function and moving courses online. That doesn't address the deeper dilemma: Training and learning are not the same thing.

In our view, training describes an outside-in approach to providing known quantifiable content, while learning describes an inside-out process that originates with the learner's desire to know, either long held or spontaneously arising from recent events or a moving interaction.

The new social learning fosters an environment where people readily and easily pick up new knowledge and skills as the world shifts around them, meeting the demands of a constantly changing mobile world.

The new social learning transcends social media, training, or workplace learning practices of the past because it offers

♦ more information sources: access to people who can lessen your uncertainty with vetted data, presentations, research, and wide perspectives that can help make your case (or your decision) easier

♦ more dissemination points: people can self-serve their needs by accessing your resources, giving you back your time and simultaneously meeting their needs

♦ an open approach to a wide network of communicators and collaborators who can help work flow.

If this is your first step into social media for learning, you are not alone. And if you're one of the veterans, please leverage these new tools and technology to share your knowledge and collaborate with us all.

Informing Decisions

Each of the next chapters begins with a case study from an organization deeply engaged in using social media to learn. We end this opening chapter, intended to provide context for the specific approaches addressed ahead, with the story of an organization using social media to offer context and make decisions clear.

Although your organization and the CIA may seem to have nothing in common, their objectives are not so different from those of every organization.

In 2006, a team of analysts at the CIA were tapped to replace an old print-based publication, primarily containing information from the president's intelligence briefing or about a crisis that had come to light. Like a newspaper, a certain amount of space was reserved for graphics and the rest was used for text. It worked, but it never shined.

Rather than build on what they already had, they started fresh, creating a new structure with social media sensibilities and a brighter vision.

The result is a daily electronic publication to update senior policy and security officials on trends and news overseas that have the potential to affect U.S. interests. The analysis in the publication is classified, noting the methods used to acquire the information and the sensitivity of the topics it contains. More than just a newspaper, it anticipates developments and makes projections about the future.

The CIA calls it *The CIA World Intelligence Review* (WIRe) because the world is what they cover, intelligence is their vocation, and review is what they do.

The WIRe is the CIA's collective and dynamic online presence. The WIRe leverages innovative tools and processes to make the richness of the CIA's content, including text, multimedia, graphics, and video, accessible wherever and whenever needed. Updated throughout the day, the WIRe's front page is dynamic and customizable, and it delivers reader-specific intelligence in a timely manner. The WIRe makes it easy to navigate volumes of reporting by linking analysis with source materials and providing robust search and feedback capabilities to support knowledge management.

For the CIA, being "central" doesn't simply reflect the title of a director, the name of the organization, or its role for legislators. It refers to *being central*, being essential to customers. The organization aims to lead the way, at the center, pioneering in times of change through demonstrating applied leadership.

In creating the WIRe, the team followed four "tracks." These objectives mirror those of many organizations pursuing a new vision:

- ◆ Retire and replace what no longer works. Get better, learn from errors, and commit to getting it right.

- ◆ Embrace the best of what's being done in the private sector and apply it to intelligence, providing it in a user-friendly, online way. Customers accustomed to the BBC.com or Google News would know how to use this.

♦ Develop a relationship with customers. Communicate with them; don't just transmit information to them. Pay attention to how they interact with the information and make data-driven improvements because of it.

♦ Recognize that we won't always know how social media tools fit or how they will apply to us, but innovation and flexibility are part of our mission, and we'll weave them into our activity.

Although these four objectives have grown over time, the team still lives by them, mindful that customers don't purchase the WIRe with money; they invest in it with their time. And invest they have. The new system has eclipsed the old system that had about 750 viewers a day. The system now has more than 100,000 registered users across the globe. It has become the gold standard for information sharing in the U.S. government. It is printed out as part of the president's briefing, read at the cabinet level, and added to and read online by sailors and soldiers implementing national security. In these ways, it's as far reaching as it is impactful.

The WIRe's purpose is to inform decisions, revealing what people think about as they make decisions. The WIRe

> *Rather than tell the story of a leader in an emerging government through words or a few static images, the WIRe can show a video clip, perhaps captured by a spectator, of how the leader whips up the crowd with a passion and a presentation style that reaches into the hearts of his audience. Now anyone seeing that clip can understand why he is so powerful.*

is the CIA's voice, expressing as an institution its perspective on a topic. Now it also provides a means to express knowledge in a collaborative space others can link to and from, add to, and learn with, so it no longer represents discrete, isolated data. It expresses personal interaction attached to relevant information that with a few clicks connects to all other relevant information. It's interconnected and put into the context of what's going on in the world.

Rather than tell the story of a leader in an emerging government through words or a few static images, the WIRe can show a video clip, perhaps captured by a spectator, of how the leader whips up the crowd with a passion and a presentation style that reaches into the hearts of his audience. Now anyone seeing that clip can understand why he is so powerful.

With that, producers of intelligence can make points more vibrantly, creating presentations with great impact. Conveying the message goes beyond basic audio, video, and text sharing. Media are integrated from multiples sources and delivered and constructed by many people. People can discover a framework of intelligence relationships and see that everything is connected, for the most accurate representation.

In addition to shared intelligence published by the WIRe team, those viewing the information create new knowledge through the paths they take in their discovery, the comments they leave, and the tags and social bookmarks they create. Each intelligence gatherer—"learner" as it were—can see what someone else navigated to or tagged from a particular point of departure, then see what else she or he tagged as relevant for making informed decisions. By observing one another's tags and navigation, people can also discover other people and groups interested in similar topics, potentially making decisions about similar things. This facilitates new relationships and new perspectives.

The WIRe becomes a combination of daily intelligence and a grouping of topics, trails of interests, and search queries, leaving an archive that can satisfy a series of needs from customers that may not exist yet. Rather than try to tailor a presentation to meet those various needs, the WIRe becomes a diamond that in its raw form has value in itself. What gives it sparkle is the ability for each decision maker, each person seeking timely information, to cut in and look at it through an individual lens, looking for different facets. It might be that the detail you want is on the homepage, the highlights presented by the WIRe team, or through an RSS feed you create and view. A regional page gives you another aspect, and topic areas a third.

What makes it unlike systems that have come before it within or outside government is that it works in seemingly conflicting worlds—that of wide-open sharing and that of the highest security. Both extremes are dangerous. As the editor-in-chief of the WIRe, Geoffrey Fowler, says, "Share too broadly, and people can die. Hold your information too closely, decisions can be ill-informed and people can die. Our responsibility is to share broadly *and* securely—to make certain that these two critical needs are not viewed as incompatible extremes. The truth of the intelligence business is that information sharing and information security need to co-exist."[26]

The WIRe provides openness and security in tandem by building on the CIA's security clearance system. Although there are restrictions, people using the system can search all the data holdings and discover trails leading to information they didn't even know existed. The organizational culture is moving from one focused exclusively on the need to know to one recognizing that success depends on the need to share. The WIRe focuses more on intelligence than the locks and walls between groups.

The CIA's ongoing interest and work with social media tools inspires us in our work. Its attention to both security and distribution reminded us as we wrote this book that systems should be facilitators for learning, not gatekeepers or megaphones. Social media can and should provide a medium for what people need now to make educated decisions. Working together, each of us, like pebbles tossed in a pond, can make both ripples and waves.

Load the boat.

Paving Online Community Roads

By enabling connections among employees, organizations can more easily offer customized work arrangements, establish virtual teams, bring new employees up to speed quickly, improve collaboration, and increase retention with people who hadn't felt a strong sense of belonging in the past.

—Patricia Romeo

D Street Leader, Deloitte

◆ ◆ ◆

Patricia Romeo didn't expect that when she joined Deloitte,* an organization whose primary assets are its people, she'd find herself missing the camaraderie, the shoptalk, and the chatter that sometimes frustrated and distracted her in previous jobs. Based in Cincinnati, Ohio, often working from a home office, Romeo missed the buzz.[1]

Apparently other Deloitte employees missed it too, because when Romeo began to investigate, she learned that thousands of people at the company were using social networking tools such as Facebook and LinkedIn to socialize and connect. Leaders in the organization were beginning to worry that these connections going on outside the firm's

*As used in this book, "Deloitte" means Deloitte LLP and its subsidiaries. Please see www.deloitte.com/us/about for a detailed description of the legal structure of Deloitte LLP and its subsidiaries.

firewall were putting Deloitte's intellectual property in the wild for others to see. For an organization that prides itself on intellectual capital, this was alarming; yet the leaders could see that employees were enthusiastic about this new way to work together. And contrary to some managers' fears, it helped rather than hindered productivity.

We start this chapter on online communities with the example of Deloitte because it's not a high-tech Silicon Valley company where you'd expect to see digital-age practices. However, it has challenges typical of many companies today—distributed teams and divisions that feel disconnected, intellectual capital that needs to be selectively shared among employees, and a workforce that is growing steadily younger and expects work to be tech enabled.

> *People at Deloitte with a natural need to connect had found Internet tools that were free, easy to use, and increasingly popular. On their own, employees were creating ad hoc communities to work faster, tap into other people's knowledge, and connect with colleagues no matter where in the world they were working. Meanwhile, Deloitte was missing out on putting these powerful tools to work for the company's benefit.*

People at Deloitte with a natural need to connect had found Internet tools that were free, easy to use, and increasingly popular. On their own, employees were creating ad hoc communities to work faster, tap into other people's knowledge, and connect with colleagues no matter where in the world they were working. Meanwhile, Deloitte was missing out on putting these powerful tools to work for the company's benefit.

Years before, Deloitte conducted extensive research about the workplace of the future. They conducted a seven-year study of demographic shifts and workforce attitude trends. They realized that "organizations of all shapes and sizes have much to learn if we are to attract and keep the talent we need to succeed. And, by the way, it's not all about the Millennials . . . it's really about everyone in the workforce." When these new challenges arose, they pointed out that there were practical ways for Deloitte to adjust their practices that would benefit everyone.[2]

The centerpiece of Deloitte's workplace of the future is an online community inside the organization's firewall, now led by Romeo. The virtual space is named "D Street" because on the main street of any town around the world, people already know the norms and conventions and can use this metaphor for being together online.

With the support of leadership and the work of the information technology, communications, and knowledge management groups, the alpha version of D Street was rolled out to 1,500 employees in mid 2007. Within months usage had surged, and it was rolled out to the rest of the organization.

The CEO of Deloitte Financial Advisory Services LLP, David Williams, articulates his vision and strategy in a D Street blog.

Chet Wood, chairman and CEO of Deloitte Tax LLP, says that, "Through D Street, I am gaining a greater perspective on what's on the minds of our people. It's provided a unique platform to engage in very personal and candid dialogue."[3]

People say they visit D Street because it makes a large organization feel smaller; they can learn about people when working with them remotely; and they can glean a little about people's likes, dislikes, hobbies, and interests as a way to help build rapport. With the virtual networking capabilities, they can feel like part of something larger than themselves or their immediate team.

The terms *online community* and *social network* are used here to define something similar. In years past, a space such as Facebook was called an online community or a web community; today spaces like D Street are often called social networks. Technically speaking, online communities allow anyone within the space access to anyone else in the space. A social network requires a connection (someone in your network) who can pave the way for you to meet someone else.

Community Capabilities

A core capability of any online community is its member profiles. Viewing a person's profile should essentially provide the same feel as visiting his or her office—complete with pictures of the kids on the desk and certifications and awards on the walls.

Rachel Happe, principal at The Community Roundtable, a peer network for community managers and social media practitioners, reinforces this point, "Communities are fundamentally about relationships of learning from peers so online communities must be created around individuals. The greater their ability to share themselves—both professionally and personally—through profiles and content tools, the greater the potential of the community to foster connections that result in business outcomes."[4]

To avoid asking for information the organization already has, profiles are pre-populated with basic details, including name, job title, and contact information from Deloitte's databases. In net vernacular, D Street is a mashup that takes existing data and combines it with employee-generated content.

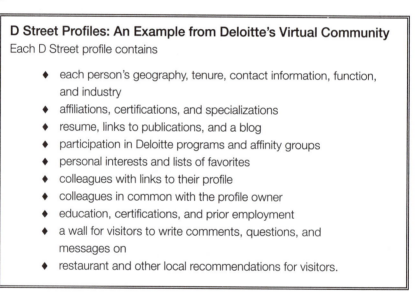

D Street Profiles: An Example from Deloitte's Virtual Community
Each D Street profile contains

- ♦ each person's geography, tenure, contact information, function, and industry
- ♦ affiliations, certifications, and specializations
- ♦ resume, links to publications, and a blog
- ♦ participation in Deloitte programs and affinity groups
- ♦ personal interests and lists of favorites
- ♦ colleagues with links to their profile
- ♦ colleagues in common with the profile owner
- ♦ education, certifications, and prior employment
- ♦ a wall for visitors to write comments, questions, and messages on
- ♦ restaurant and other local recommendations for visitors.

Profiles are enhanced by their searchability. Because they include the industry and sector each person focuses on, they provide a way for people to quickly find a French-speaking health specialist or a Spanish-speaking logistician. Employees can personalize their profiles with photographs and supplement them with links to their Facebook and LinkedIn profiles. A profile can even include content a person has written if it's in the organization's knowledge management system. This feature has led to an uptick in people sharing content with the knowledge management team.

D Street also enables people to introduce colleagues to one another, list external social network memberships, and write blogs. They can leave comments and search for others who share their interests. For example, an employee who searches on "Enterprise 2.0" will find other people interested in that topic as well as information about how to connect. If people want to connect with parents of twins or a Hispanic employee network in the Midwest, they can do that with a few keystrokes.

New hires can easily find five people who went to the same college they did, three who worked for the same company, and two who grew up in their small town. Whenever someone with a similar history joins the organization, he or she can get an alert. With the ability to make these kinds of connections, cold and impersonal quickly turns warm and welcoming.

Communities Face Forward

A research program at IBM's Institute for Knowledge-Based Organizations, further supported by work done between The Network Roundtable led by Rob Cross at the University of Virginia and Bill Kahn of Boston University, consistently found that better-connected people enjoy substantial performance, learning, and decision-making benefits. The research showed that people use communities to find others who provide resources, career development, personal support, and context. The depth and breadth of these relationships, whether they are serendipitous or planned, predicts performance, innovation, employee commitment, and job satisfaction.[5]

Jamie Pappas, community manager for EMC's internal online community, EMC|ONE, says that her favorite part of the job is "connecting people who might have never crossed paths, let alone learned valuable lessons from each other, exchanging information that makes their lives easier and enabling them to enjoy more of the things they are passionate about."[6]

Community, the place where we live, work, and do things with other people, is a concept most of us learned and put into use when we were very young. Coming from two Latin words meaning "with gifts," the term *community* suggests a general sense of reciprocity, altruism, and benefit that comes from doing something together. The old town of Mombasa, Kenya; the Green Bay Packers fans who watch games wearing cheese-wedge hats; or jugglers worldwide are all examples of communities. Each type has its own shared language, rituals, customs, and collective memory. In most cases, sharing is the norm and people choose what information they share.

> *Because online communities are not constrained by the need for anyone's physical presence, we have greater flexibility with our ability to join, learn, and congregate with people who have similar interests no matter their location.*

When people speak of community in today's hustle-and-bustle world, they are usually calling up a hope of reviving the closer bonds among people that seemed to occur in ages past. Don Cohen and Larry Prusak, authors of *In Good Company: How Social Capital Makes Organizations Work*, point out that when we talk about community in business, we nod to the reality that companies and the individuals who run them don't exist in a social vacuum devoid of ties, histories, loyalties, and values that might influence their actions. There is also a similarity between the way people have learned in communities throughout time and how people in organizations learn.[7]

Because online communities are not constrained by the need for anyone's physical presence, we have greater flexibility with our ability to join, learn, and congregate with people who have similar interests no matter their location.

As such, community can be a value itself; a joining together that offers the benefits of belonging, commitment, mutuality, and trust. These are environments where people are free to learn.

We've been working side by side with people since sandbox days, but there were limits to how much and how far we could share. Some of us went to schools where talking to each other was discouraged. Some of us went to work for bosses who made it clear that talking to co-workers was not real work. And most of us were on our own when it came to learning on the job.

Local area networks opened an era for communication software such as email, instant messaging, and Lotus Notes databases. We were still separated by walls, but we began reaching beyond them to share what we were doing, ask questions, post details, and mingle our ideas online.

These tools became the means by which people started contributing to a body of knowledge. Few of us had the time to write or post to a knowledge management system about all that we were doing, and when we did it was hard for others to access, let alone use.

Out of these challenges grew the idea of turning everything into objects, bits, or clusters of information that could be reused to build something else. With standardized shapes and sizes, you can assemble almost anything you need.

Yet this still left out tacit knowledge—things that are hard to communicate by writing and speaking but can be learned by watching others and actually doing them. What people crave is the opportunity to learn from one another, side by side, gaining both hard facts and in-context wisdom. What else could account for the sustained use of classroom learning decades beyond a time when people realized its inherent limits? We value an opportunity to see we are not alone; there are people we can lean on, learn from, interact with, and rely on to help us.

In a landmark study, Richard J. Light of the Harvard Graduate School of Education discovered that one of the strongest determinants of students' success in higher education—more important than their instructors' teaching styles—was their ability to form or participate in small study groups. People who studied in groups, even once a week, were more engaged in their studies, were better prepared for class, and learned significantly more than students who worked on their own.[8]

The demographics research at Deloitte uncovered something similar: People who could look to other people online for support felt more connected than their nonconnected counterparts, stayed with their employer longer, and produced stronger results.[9] The creators of Deloitte's D Street recognized the benefits of nurturing a culture of reciprocal learning.

Make a Case for Online Communities

Online communities can bridge the gap between the climate you have at work today and the one you want to foster—one in which people want to learn from each other because they trust one another. They want to hear from people like them, facing the same decisions, the same challenges, and the same options. As Babe Ruth once said, "You may have the greatest bunch of individual stars in the world, but if they don't play together, the club won't be worth a dime." The way the team plays collectively determines its success.

Rather than use online communities to duplicate programs and processes that work, look at your organization's weaknesses. According to Harvard Business School professor Mikolaj Jan Piskorski, online communities are most useful when they address failures in the operation of offline communities.[10]

Although what follows isn't a complete list of challenges that individuals and organizations want to overcome, it represents some of the most common concerns they face.

Put Knowledge to Use

Sabre Holdings, the company that owns Travelocity and several other global travel reservation systems, created an internal online community—SabreTown—that facilitates learning and communication in ways that address many of the issues holding other companies back.

"The goal was to provide an internal tool for professional networking so that employees could connect quickly and easily," says Erik Johnson, general manager of the software underpinning SabreTown. At the time the networking tool was created, Sabre Holdings had grown from a small U.S. operation into one with 10,000 employees in 59 countries, many telecommuting and beginning to feel disconnected from colleagues and information.[11]

To use SabreTown, employees complete a profile of their interests and expertise. When someone posts a question to an online bulletin board, the system's predictive modeling software automatically sends it to the 15 people whose expertise is most relevant to the question. The more people who complete profiles and the more questions that are asked and answered, the better the inference engine is able to assign questions appropriately.

"You have a greater chance of getting a useful answer if your question is directed not just to the people you already know, but to the people who have the most relevant knowledge," explains Johnson.

SabreTown is credited with substantial savings for the company. It identified $500,000 in direct savings the first year, but based on anecdotal results, that figure doesn't come close to representing the total savings. Johnson attributes the site's success partly to the fact that management ceded control over its use to line employees. He says, "A big benefit for us is that SabreTown is effectively creating a massive knowledge base that employees willingly populate with their own information."

"The more you can know about the people you work with, and what they value and don't value," says Ric Merrifield, Microsoft business scientist and author of *Rethink*, "the easier it is to get targeted and tailored messages to them, providing them something valuable."[12]

Stay Current, Be Aware

A common measure of employee satisfaction is to what extent people feel they know what's going on in the company. This is partly a measure of how well leadership communicates. It is also representative of how much information is shared among employees, and that's a slippery slope. We all want to keep up with work going on around us, but few of us have time to learn from other people at work, let alone share what we are doing ourselves.

This is where online communities play a growing role. Their search tools help you find people you want to learn from and send you automatic updates when their work overlaps with yours. Microsharing, blogs, and even profiles can provide quick ways to update others and be updated in real time, giving these communities a sense of immediacy you don't get even with email. Online communities create ambient awareness, which is what social scientists call this sort of incessant online contact. It is, they say, very much like being physically near someone and picking up on his or her mood through actions—body language, sighs, stray comments—out of the corner of your eye.

Clive Thompson, science, technology, and culture writer for *Wired* and *The New York Times Magazine*, calls this "the *paradox* of ambient awareness. Each little update—each individual bit of social information—is insignificant on its own, even supremely mundane. But taken together, over time, the little snippets coalesce into a surprisingly sophisticated portrait of your colleagues' lives, like thousands of dots making a pointillist painting. The ambient information becomes 'a type of ESP,' an invisible dimension floating over us.[13]

Clay Shirky, author of *Here Comes Everybody* and *Cognitive Surplus* refers to "algorithmic authority," meaning that if many people are pointing to the same thing at the same time, it's probably worth paying attention to.[14]

Does constant updating sound like a bunch of busybodies with nothing better to do? Paula Thornton, an enterprise 2.0 architect and designer points out, "In the machine world no one would imagine doing away with the conveyor belt. Updates are the conveyor belts of information in a service organization."[15]

That conveyer belt of information should be interesting to any organization with a large distributed workforce because it supports the dynamics, efficiency, and agility of a small company. It raises awareness of others within an organization and, with this, opportunities for learning, collaboration, and innovation.

Online spaces rich in ambient information increase the quantity of tacit knowledge shared because they make you aware of what people are doing in a way that was not possible before.

Contribute to the Conversation

It takes new employees, on average, nine months to feel they know enough about their jobs and their new organization to be willing to contribute in a collaborative way. By that time, many of their best insights as newcomers (having what Buddhists call the "Beginner's Mind") and their practical experience from having worked elsewhere are far from fresh.

What about people who are wicked smart and do great work, but just aren't inclined to share what they know or what they're working on? Think of the increased brainshare if they had a venue they felt comfortable contributing to.

Online exchanges give employees an opportunity to increase their visibility in the company and allow management to identify talent they might never have been aware of.

Consulting firm Booz Allen Hamilton created hello.bah.com, an internal portal with online community capabilities, to enable employees to blog, participate in wikis, locate mentors, build their brands as subject matter experts, network with colleagues in offices across the United States—and have fun in the process. Because many of the firm's employees do not work full time from a Booz Allen office, the online space is all about connection, says associate Megan Murray. "Hello.bah.com removes geographic boundaries, which is especially important to new hires and those working on client sites. It takes connections within the firm and makes them visible, so you can find good information quickly and hit the ground running on your first day."[16]

Best Buy's internal community, BlueShirt Nation, was first envisioned as a site to harvest marketing ideas from people who work in their stores. "The promise of being able to go out and tap into 140,000 employees and use computer magic to do it was really attractive to us," said Gary Koelling, who heads the online space.[17] Once employees were connected, the site began filling with ideas and discussions that reached far beyond marketing. For instance, when one employee posted his thoughts on why it would be beneficial for all full-time employees to have email access, it sparked a conversation that eventually led to a shift in policy to enable just that. Loop Marketplace is a location on the site where employees can post ideas and management can harvest them.

Online communities prompt real-time dialogue between employees and management, adding a degree of transparency to an organization that couldn't have existed before. It allows employees to actively take responsibility for shaping or re-shaping their organization.

Create Opportunities to Reflect

Social media, by its nature and even its name, implies an outward connection. Look out. Look up. Look around. What about looking in? Online communities offer intrapersonal benefits for those paying attention to what they can learn about themselves.

Although the public visibility of an online community can be unsettling, there is a very positive result of incessant updating: a culture of people who know much more about themselves. Many of the people we spoke with about their social media use described an unexpected side effect of self-discovery. Stopping several times a day to observe what you're feeling or thinking can become, after weeks and weeks, a sort of philosophical act. It's like the Zen concept of mindfulness.

Having an online audience for self-reflection can prompt people to work harder at it and describe it more accurately in more interesting ways—the status update as a literary form.

Laura Fitton, founder of oneforty and co-author of *Twitter for Dummies*, points out that her constant status updating has even made her "a happier person, a calmer person" because the process of, say, describing a horrid morning at work forces her to look at it objectively. "It drags you out of your own head," she says.[18] In an age of virtual awareness, perhaps the person you see most clearly will be yourself.

Who do you influence? Look through the people who have written in your guest book or chosen to follow what you're writing, and you'll begin to get a picture of who takes an interest in the areas you focus on. Someone you have admired for a long time may be looking at what you do; someone you'd never considered talking with about a topic near to your heart might be chiming in when you don't expect it.

Someone who follows you may consistently ask you to clarify or dig deeper into theory when you explain something. This may help improve your writing or steer your work to be more practical.

Establish Trust

Trust in any relationship, organizational or personal, is only earned over time through actions. People require some level of trust before they are willing or able to learn something from another person. Each of us seeks ways to determine if we can trust the people we work with enough to count on what they share.

Online community fosters relationships with people across multiple service lines, geographic locations, and affiliations. You can build and earn trust with people you may not have encountered before.

Sociologists have researched trust in communities extensively. They have identified that ongoing positive interaction, getting a sense of someone's "identity," and noting people's opinions of others are keys to gaining trust.

Getting to know one another before meeting face to face fosters authenticity and gives trust a head start. It's as if we've known the person for a long time and can jump right into working with them, learning from them, and getting on with whatever we got together to do. Quick and constant updates that create ambient awareness accumulate over time, and we begin to trust and show we're trustworthy.

Online community fosters relationships with people across multiple service lines, geographic locations, and affiliations. You can build and earn trust with people you may not have encountered before.

Trusting people also helps us work with them across the miles. People at IBM, Deloitte, and practically every organization we spoke with talked of the ease with which people join virtual teams where they can create a baseline of comfort with other people on the team before they begin their work.

Building trust increases group efficiency and enables conflict resolution. Cliff Figallo, author of *Hosting Web Communities: Building Relationships, Increasing Customer Loyalty, and Maintaining a Competitive Edge,* said it beautifully, "Trust is the social lubricant that makes community possible."[19] And it allows learning to happen in communities.

Trust in a relationship determines in large part how effectively you can learn from a person. In a trusting relationship, you're likely to listen to and believe what the other person is saying; that is, we trust his or her competence and will allow him or her to influence our thinking. Trusted relationships also give us the freedom to ask questions that reveal our lack of knowledge because we trust the person's goodwill toward us. More than just a nicety, building trust in networks has a great deal to do with our individual ability to learn and the ability of an entire organization to learn and improve.

Inform Decisions

Good decisions are the heart and soul of any successful, fast-moving enterprise, and the more informed the decision, the better it is likely to be. Although most people say they want input from co-workers prior to making a decision, often it's just too hard to do in a timely manner. Real-time input on decisions is yet another way that online communities facilitate what people learn. Being able to access tacit knowledge from a wide range of people in the enterprise and beyond allows us to solicit opinions; ask questions; get pointers to more information; and see referrals, testimonials, benchmarking, and updates that relate to what we need to decide.

In an IBM case study, Robin Spencer, senior research fellow at Pfizer, says that her company's online community allows it to reach across organizational silos and leverage more organizational wisdom than previously possible. It means Pfizer now drives faster and better decisions and shortens time to market, which helps keep the company at the forefront of its changing industry.[20]

Pfizer's social media efforts began with managers asking permission to talk to researchers on teams other than their own. This created an atmosphere of permission where it's assumed to be OK to reach out and ask.

The community becomes a hub for the viral distribution of knowledge. You can see how many of your colleagues recommended a research source or a video from a conference on the other side of the world, or who have simply joined a conversation. And in turn they are benchmarking against one another to determine if the actions they are taking are the right ones and if their decisions are well informed.

Pfizer also created "challenges," social jam sessions in which hundreds or even thousands of researchers weigh in on issues. Spencer emphasized that in addition to harnessing all the research stored in people's memories, the method also shoots problems "sideways through organizational silos," which previously were not sharing knowledge effectively.

Learn New Technology

It sometimes seems like keeping up with new technology is a full-time job. No sooner have we mastered some software application than a new version comes out, pushing us behind the curve. Organizations face this problem on a huge scale as work becomes more virtual all the time and the supporting technology multiplies like fruit flies.

Too often organizations take a "not on our dime" approach to helping employees learn to use new tools. "Want to learn all this new-fangled stuff? That's what weekends are for!"

Yet, research into experiential learning shows there is no better way to learn how to do something than by doing it. If you know the people in your organization are going to need to be proficient in working online and collaborating with co-workers in more virtual ways, there is no better place to learn how than by working there now. As a new and emerging set of tools, social networking requires a degree of experimentation. People have to try different approaches, see what feels comfortable to them, and get a return that encourages them to continue.

A customer can form impressions of the company from a phone call, a website, a retail counter, a reservation agent, or any number of other experiences. Kate Frohling, senior vice president of brand management at Wells Fargo, says, "To make employees not just advocates for the corporate culture, but to help them all speak with 'our voice,' it's essential to make customer conversations part of Wells Fargo's training. The customer's experience is our top priority, and we want it to be consistent."[21]

This includes familiarity with the digital tools that employees will be using with customers. Blogging, emailing, tweeting, texting, and using an internal social networking site are part of Wells Fargo's employee training programs.

To get as many people as possible ready for social media tools, the consumer innovation team at Humana created a series of self-guided training modules for employees to learn about various social media tools without becoming overwhelmed. People can spend a little time each day to get up to speed and gain a sense of how these resources can help them. "LinkedIn in 15 Minutes a Day," for instance, gives employees a chance to learn enough to test it on their own. Other 15-minute courses introduce the basics of Twitter, YouTube, and Facebook. The team has also created modules on subjects such as RSS feeds and readers, blogging, search engine optimization, and social marketing campaigns. They post these modules in an online community-like space called the Social Media Commons, designed specifically as a place where people can practice and learn.

Respond to Critics

One of the largest roadblocks to getting started with online communities is those who think they are not a good idea. Here are the most common objections we hear and ways we believe you can address them.

Our Management Team Will Never Sign Off on This

Few people agree to new things they don't understand or see value in. Consider going through the list of challenges presented earlier in the chapter, pull out those you know your organization needs to fix most, and frame your case by explaining how an online community could help meet those goals.

A customer can form impressions of the company from a phone call, a website, a retail counter, a reservation agent, or any number of other experiences. To make employees not just advocates for the corporate culture, but to help them speak with your voice, make customer conversations part of your training.

People you work with may already see benefit in such a community but don't know how to proceed. By explaining your interest, you might open the door to getting started.

A corporate study from the Society for New Communication Research, called the "Tribalization of Business," found that the greatest obstacles to making a community work were not about technology or getting funding, but about getting people involved in the community (51 percent), finding enough time to manage the community (45 percent), and attracting people to the community (34 percent).[22] Management was not cited as an obstacle. Just 9 percent of the respondents said that their management was unwilling to share with community members or support the initiative.

Lois Kelly, a Beeline Labs partner and one of the Tribalization report researchers, pointed out that a common fear—losing control—"may not be as big an issue as [people] think. Clearly the bigger challenge is focusing the community around a purpose that people want to contribute to and be involved with—and devoting the right resources to promote and support the community."

People Will Waste Precious Time, Which Isn't Good for Business or the Bottom Line

In tough economic times, some people seem to become critical of every activity, even those generating the energy required for success. In large part, innovation and learning comes from the little moments between the activities we've previously thought of as the "real" work.

When people accuse social media tools of causing productivity problems, do a quick reality check with them about the methods people around your organization use to communicate, collaborate, and learn today. Detractors will probably find they are fundamentally social.

Time spent in online communities needs to be managed, but the same could be said about time on the telephone, using email, or in meetings. The challenge may be more about how to address some people's compulsion to constantly look busy rather than get their work done.

In our research, we saw time and again that the earliest adopters of social media tools are technically savvy people who were already having these conversations, just not as easily or with such strong results. They were the ones on their phones, on email discussion lists, in bulletin boards, or talking it up with the people in their physical proximity.

Social media, including online communities, didn't spawn this behavior. People seeking the next great *aha* weren't the wallflowers who kept to themselves. They were social enough already to know they did their best when engaged with other people.

If someone has an addiction to being online, he or she is likely to be a poor performer because of that addictive trait. In general though, even a little leisure browsing has been shown to help sharpen workers' concentration because they have had some downtime to relax and broaden their thinking.

Josh Bancroft, technology evangelist and blogger at Intel, tells of an experience when one of the people he worked with needed to accomplish a task. To do so, she needed to use a piece of software no one in her group had ever heard of, let alone knew enough about to use. It would have taken months to learn the software and complete the task. Instead, she searched the organization's internal wiki system and found someone who had done a project using the software. She contacted that person and asked for help. Within a matter of weeks the project was done.[23] How many wiki pages was the efficiency gain worth? Add up not only the time saved by one person, but also the advantages of a quicker time to market for this project.

> *Many employees have already integrated technology into their lives. Their ability to connect serves them and their employers well. While their colleagues waste time in meetings or engage in long phone conversations, they sum things up in quick messages over their microsharing system.*

Many employees have already integrated technology into their lives. Their ability to connect serves them and their employers well. While their colleagues waste time in meetings or engage in long phone conversations, they sum things up in quick messages over their microsharing system. And given their networks of online connections, they discover people who can become true friends or valued business colleagues—people they wouldn't have been able to find in the pre-Internet era.

Do people fulfill their work objectives or not? Are they getting their jobs done? If so, why should anyone care if they're spending time in the online community? By being there, they create relationships and create their own place in the company. By getting to know other people in the company, they're getting to know the company better.

Employees Will Give Away Company Secrets

People form their own communities with or without organizational support. It's hard to monitor and control information and content that employees put out on the Internet, but it doesn't mean they're not doing it.

If you create a space for people to work in, learn from, and engage with, you provide them a viable way to work that doesn't involve going around the system.

Many organizational leaders we spoke with said their employees became more efficient and easier to monitor (and influence) when there was a private forum for sharing ideas, information, and work tasks. These spaces brought people together, and they began to work more as a unit without any suggestive pushing from management.

Most companies track how many people use the communities and how often and which sub-sites and topics get the most traffic. This allows site managers to make improvements based on real behavior. At the Intercontinental Hotel Group, for example, the Leaders Lounge is constantly tweaked—based on actual usage—to replace content created by the learning team with content generated by the managers using the site.

Some People Will Just Lurk

It's OK if some people just lurk. The silent majority who rarely make the time to post can still gain tremendous value from the breadth of the organization they can glimpse online. They can learn from those participating more actively. In communities with tools that automatically recommend content based on what others read, lurkers become contributors without even having to chime in.

Recommendations

Now it's your turn to listen, watch, and learn from your physical community and consider if people will be willing to take some of their work online.

Jamie Pappas at EMC offers the following recommendations to anyone interested in deploying social media for their organization.[24]

Look Inward

Although many organizations have begun to adopt outward-facing social media strategies, putting social capabilities on their externally facing websites, there are advantages to beginning inside first. EMC | ONE was launched to drive employee proficiency with social media tools and provide EMC employees an introduction to a new way of working. Available to all EMC employees, contractors, and vendors who have signed a nondisclosure agreement with EMC, it provides a place to understand and become comfortable with social media tools and terminology among friends and colleagues. EMC did this before launching external communities so that people inside the company would be prepared for that next level of engagement with business partners, prospects, and customers.

Differentiate Benefits

You can't sell the same value proposition to every group. What works for telemarketing is not likely to work for programming. Take time to understand the group you're talking to and adapt the message, making it relevant to them. Don't just say social media is great. Tell people how it benefits them, how it can broaden their unique networks and enable them to do new things. Tailoring your message to your audience is at the heart of enabling them to see value in the new tools and the new ways of working being proposed.

Welcome Everyone

With social media tools, each person has an opportunity to provide his or her distinctive perspective on a broad range of topics. Everyone in an organization, regardless of role, title, or focus, can contribute insights to the conversation. The more people that come together, the more information is shared, the more ideas are generated, and the better informed people's decisions can be. All of this discussing and collaborating together leads to an invaluable online, searchable resource for everyone who participates.

"I cannot think of a time during my 20 years at EMC when I felt more informed, involved, and confident in myself and the business before EMC|ONE."
— John Walton, Symmetrix Engineer and EMC Fellow[25]

Be Aware That It's Not All Business

Organizations often want to offer their employees a community or social media toolset but don't want the conversations to wander off specific business themes. As social creatures, people thrive on meaningful connections with other people. Although most conversations should have a professional focus, connections across topics build relationships and trust sometimes more effectively than sticking solely to job-related areas. Pappas shares, "In EMC | ONE, the restaurant recommendations wiki is one of our most popular and serves to bring people together cross-departmentally and cross-geographically who would not have otherwise had an opportunity to connect. It serves as an excellent icebreaker and provides employees an opportunity to share their unique perspectives in a way that is not intimidating, especially for those new to the organization. People begin their relationship by sharing a recommendation, and the interaction ultimately facilitates their ability to learn about other perspectives and talents across the organization from other contributors. It has also become a hot resource for the sales people visiting headquarters, as it provides them with a starting point for where to dine or take customers, partners, or prospects who visit EMC."

Do Important Work

Burt Kaliski, director of EMC's Innovation Network, and his team started planning for the company's annual Innovation Conference by brainstorming ideas about the focus of the event on EMC | ONE. As that was settled, the team moved on to posting and refining event details. Then they launched their innovation submission process on EMC | ONE and received more than 900 submissions from passionate EMC employees all over the world who felt so comfortable in the community that they were even eager to post their submissions on the site for others to review, comment on, and provide suggestions.[26]

Listen and Prepare for Possible Objections and Concerns

You will not convince anyone to join the online community by ignoring or dismissing critics. By listening, you may find opportunities for improvements, further exploration, or even education on misinformation or lack of knowledge or understanding. If you can anticipate and think of a response to some of the objections ahead of time, you may be able to keep the conversation on point, and it will help you to illustrate the benefits for that group with meaningful examples and case studies.

Share the Love

The atmosphere of any community provides much of what new members need to know about what they can expect there. If there are too many rules, people are discouraged from participating or they fear their participation won't be accepted because it's not sanctioned content. If there are no guidelines, people are discouraged because they don't know what is considered fair game. But, if you have a community with open-minded and welcoming members, others will feel comfortable jumping in and contributing their own insights.

Encourage Champions

Some people will naturally become advocates of the online community and social media initiatives in your organization. Welcome these people and make it easy for them to share their knowledge, experiences, and expertise with others. EMC | ONE has a voluntary mentor program that encourages people to add their names to a list of people whom anyone can contact for assistance, advice, or brainstorming. Champions have emerged from all parts of the organization, so they have the diversity of experience to share what works and what doesn't in different parts of the company and with customers, partners, and the larger ecosystem the organization serves.

The open and real-time nature of social media tools makes it essential to embed education into the roadmap of launching an enterprise initiative. If organizations want people to use social media responsibly and on behalf of the organization, they must set forth what they consider to be the "rules of engagement" and highlight examples of how people use the tools in alignment with the strategy. EMC has created a robust set of frequently asked questions, tutorials, best-practice guides, and 101 introductory modules that serve as a starting point and lay the framework for employees to feel a bit more comfortable engaging. EMC has also included social media awareness and best practices in its new hire training, so employees are aware of the guidance from the outset.

Foster Teamwork

There is no magic formula for how many people, or what departments, or what levels must be involved for people to learn through social media. Be open to exploring the right mix for your organization and be open to changing that mix frequently until the team is right for your organization's needs.

All of this makes the case that a point person (or people) coordinates the company's social media efforts beyond the tools provided for use. It also makes the case that social media success requires a team of diverse and committed people to serve the interests of not only the individuals who use it, but also the organization as a whole.

At EMC, the Social Media Advisory Council brings together the people responsible for setting and executing the social media strategy for their organization or geography. The council comprises a cross-functional, cross-geographical team of people who meet virtually on a monthly basis to collaborate on the company's social strategy, exchange ideas and best practices, solve challenges, and work together to increase awareness of social media in the organization.

"Embarking on a community initiative is not easy and requires patience and hard work to succeed—but it's a worthy pursuit," says Pappas. "Clearly define your goals and take a keen interest in the individual business needs of your audiences. Then commit to developing true partnerships with employees and stakeholders, leveraging the people who have a true passion for community and collaboration as your strongest advocates. If you do this, understanding that flexibility and change are must-have ingredients, you will find the support you need to continue to pave the road that will provide your organization with benefits you have only just begun to imagine."

Share Stories Around, Up, and Out

"People are tied together by anecdotes, impressions, observations, and narratives, which together map the shape and substance of their world. Then community becomes a diverse garden of connected stories; the more deeply people know the stories, the more deeply people know the community."

—Dan Pontefract
Senior Director of Learning, TELUS

♦ ♦ ♦

U p you climb. Fixing the telephone line for a customer who has been without service for hours. He's called customer service twice. You've done this a hundred times. But this time the weather is worse than usual. A tree is precariously close to the pole. Something just doesn't feel right. It's not as though there's someone else who could get to this remote site whom you could ask how to proceed.

You walk back to your truck, get out your handheld video camera, point it toward the pole, and narrate the situation. Three minutes later you upload the digital footage to your company's in-house learning and collaboration system, and you ask for eyes. You're feeling a little better already, knowing you're not alone. If two minds are better than one, why not thousands?

Within 10 minutes, colleagues from across the country have commented. One pointed out a wiring issue you hadn't noticed. Another suggested a new technique she'd used that you hadn't heard about. The third reminded you of a similar sticky situation you'd been in and how your instincts helped you through.

Imaginative serial or on-the-job, real-time learning? If you work for TELUS, the Vancouver, Canada–headquartered telecommunications company, this is more than science fiction.

> *By equipping technicians with a media mindset and a culture of collaboration, everyone shares responsibility for educating one another and giving each person an opportunity to seek focused help. The workforce becomes the organization's lifeline to what's happening in the field right now.*

Dan Pontefract, senior director of learning and collaboration, was hired by TELUS for the express purpose of modernizing the training function into a media-rich and customer-focused change engine. Rather than develop an expensive proprietary system, he sought out publicly available technologies and spent his budget creating a useful and highly usable system—TELUS Xchange.[1]

At its core, it is a means for the 35,000 people employed by TELUS around the world to tell stories that instruct and to seek assistance from their peers. The TELUS market consists of four categories of telecommunications access: landlines, wireless, satellite, and digital. They service 11.8 million customer connections across Canada and 12 countries around the globe.

The frontline workers need quick information nuggets, accessible from their trucks while on site with customers, to learn quickly as they change routers, set up home phone systems, and perform custom installations they may never have done before.

By equipping technicians with a media mindset and a culture of collaboration, everyone shares responsibility for educating one another and giving each person an opportunity to seek focused help. The workforce becomes the organization's lifeline to what's happening in the field right now.

No one expects the videos that employees create in the field to be spectacular Martin Scorsese productions. Value comes from their timeliness and ability to capture setting and context. People can easily upload their films, including bits of text and a few tags that let others find them easily. In cases where the video could serve a larger or more specialized audience, a small team can do postproduction editing, turning the videos into glossier shows.

People can make and review comments, rate the videos "thumbs up" or "thumbs down," and offer recommendations to other team members.

The learning and collaboration system also has the capacity to archive and serve other content including documents, recorded broadcasts, and simulations. At TELUS they also use Microsoft Live Meeting for live webcasts and virtual meetings that are then recorded, WebEx for virtual instructor-led sessions, and Cisco Telepresence units to give the sense that people are in a room together. These technologies are used most for team meetings and virtual coaching sessions.

Videos and non-video content created by Pontefract's team can be searched by topic, category, or keyword. There is a formal taxonomy and an informal "folksonomy" (a term coined by information architect, Thomas Vander Wal, combining the terms "folk" and "taxonomy" to convey an organic, ad hoc, and friendly way to tag, categorize, and locate content based on the terms people use themselves).[2] For example, a video of a TELUS TV installation could be tagged as relating to the satellite TV business, installations, TV, and wiring.

This defies any preconceived idea of who is a producer and who is a consumer of learning at TELUS. The organization's goal is to build workforce competence and acumen, enabling everyone to make good judgments and quick decisions to better serve customers.

Pontefract's organization is responsible for this vision under the banner "Learning 2.0." It supports TELUS staff when and where needed and includes virtual schools of technology, business, and leadership where all content is readily available in an easily contributed and consumed format.

Videos are used often in the TELUS school of technology and have begun being used for business and leadership training. They include those made in house and those from external sources. For example, inside TELUS Xchange is a video of John Chambers, CEO of Cisco, discussing the benefits of a networked and connected organization, which is used as part of the core leadership–learning path. Prior to creating the Learning 2.0 vision, TELUS training was predominantly classroom based or delivered through e-learning. Seventy percent was developed or delivered by outside vendors. Several business units also had their own independent training teams, precluding any chance for a cohesive vision of change.

> *Videos are used often in the TELUS school of technology and have begun being used for business and leadership training. They include those made in house and those from external sources.*

Like large and even mid-size organizations, TELUS had an array of technology related to learning: knowledge management systems; several learning management systems; an ERP system; performance review systems; and technology for wikis, blogs, podcasts, vodcasts, intranets, extranets, and other information-sharing tools.

Pontefract's first point of change was to create a common unified interface in the organization where people could tell their stories, learn, and collaborate. After 12 years of running large organizations, he knew that the first things to prompt cultural shift are the stories people tell one another. It's why media sharing is so central to his plans.

He knew the culture transformation would require more than adding an interface and tools. His team needed to change their own practices, too. For example, they decided to shut down their standalone learning management systems (LMS) because it equated learning with instructor led and e-learning events. Instead they added LMS-like features into TELUS Xchange. It is a storytelling, learning content engine, created by the organization and its members, with video as its face.

The broader TELUS community self-selects what's valuable and relevant and what's not. This is where the new journey begins.

Pictures Make Progress

Sharing stories using visuals isn't new. Pictures on rocks and cave walls date as far back as 40,000 years. Even before our predecessors congregated in communities, they drew pictures to tell narratives that conveyed movement and meaning and passed on wisdom across space and time. These stories allowed us to evolve by communicating key details and messages not as easily carried along through other means.

With quality video cameras dropping in price and video capabilities now built into more mobile devices, our ability to share still and moving images has expanded from down the path to around the world. We can now see faces and activities almost as easily as we can hear voices over the phone. Storytelling, which has always been central to the human condition, now travels across new forms of media to help us learn from one another and connect.

Anything that can be digitized can be accessed and distributed on the Internet or an intranet. Videos, audio files, podcasts, slideshows, and digital pictures can all be used to improve business processes and collaboration. As bandwidth increases and compression algorithms improve, a migration from text-based content to full-motion video ensues. At the same time, more powerful, compact, and mobile access devices make it easier to find and learn from relevant content whenever it's needed.

In the past, only businesses with deep pockets and the right technology could bring corporate stories to life, broadcast time-sensitive news to all employees, reach people in far-flung locations, and generally increase the impact of what they convey.

Organizations of all sizes can now afford the technology to stream video directly to employees' desktops. No longer do they need to rely on business satellite networks or on distributing content on VHS tapes or DVDs in the vague hope employees will make the effort to watch them.

They can be full of rich stories and ad hoc video clips from the field, or they can be little online updates throughout the day—Headline News Network style—replacing a daily newsletter as stories are blogged, tweeted, and commented on online, by anyone.

Media sharing is more than a tool or a broadcast medium. It's more than the multimedia CD-ROMs of years past. It's a way to foster interaction and sociability, another way to cultivate community—a community that extends to co-workers, partners, suppliers, customers, and other people interacting in the workplace. Media sharing opens new opportunities to interact, share, produce, and collaborate.

Videos communicate in a powerful and succinct way. Images work better than print or digital text to convey vision. Watching a mechanic assemble an engine can be more valuable than reading 10 books on the topic. Video engages your eyes, ears, and imagination to help you picture yourself solving a problem.

> *Videos communicate in a powerful and succinct way. Images work better than print or digital text to convey vision. Watching a mechanic assemble an engine can be more valuable than reading 10 books on the topic. Video engages your eyes, ears, and imagination to help you picture yourself solving a problem.*

People-powered content provides buzz and insight. As more people walk around with camera-enabled smartphones and install webcams and microphones, employee-generated content will offer great insights to companies.

Phyllis Myers, producer of the NPR radio show *Fresh Air*, characterized viral video as a "sharing experience" instead of the old "shared experience" that broadcast networks and publishers typically offer. Rather than waiting for interesting content from media giants, people increasingly reach out to pull content they want.

They can find a broad assortment of free videos from commercial sites, including YouTube and Vimeo, and your organization's clips from in-house–focused software such as Altus.

If a picture is worth a thousand words, moving pictures on an endless array of topics are priceless. A bottom-up approach to employee-generated video means that just about anything related to your organization can and will be captured and shared. Furthermore, the YouTube factor, where people celebrate wacky and compelling stories, means as long as video is interesting and authentic, homegrown will often do. As many podcasters have already found out, content is more important than presentation. If you have something to say that is relevant and genuinely interesting, people will watch.

Social Media Is Compelling

In an age of too much digital noise and not enough value, getting and holding attention is pivotal if you want people to learn. If you can't get people's interest, what's the point in even trying to connect with them? Old-school ways of communicating with employees and customers are often ignored altogether in the engaging and entertaining social media world.

Although some argue that social media keeps people from paying attention, research shows that it can be a big part of the solution.

A survey of more than 60 executives by Thomas Davenport and John Beck at the Accenture Institute for Strategic Change looked at what got their attention over a one-week period.[3] Overall, in rank order, the factors most highly associated with getting attention were

1. The message is *personalized*.
2. It evoked an *emotional* response.
3. It came from a *trustworthy* source or respected sender.
4. It was *concise*.

Social media excels at all of these factors. Messages that both evoked emotion and were personalized were more than twice as likely to generate a response.

The best ideas for improving your business often come from employees, partners, and customers because they have a vested interest in your success and know your organization best. Harnessing their collective wisdom through videos is both compelling and attention getting.

Media sharing encourages and enables a community where people can see and learn from one another and get contributions from everyone. Video messages that allow for comments help bridge the gap between leaders and the larger ecosystem. People can provide feedback, ask questions, and send their own videos through the platform's commenting, tagging, and sharing features.

For example, an employee who is planning to retire could create videos about her areas of expertise. A senior executive could create mentoring videos, giving advice to newcomers. A technical employee could create a step-by-step video to explain a procedure. The training department could ask employees to create videos to incorporate into a learning program.

Videos are especially good at presenting things sequentially (this happened, then that) and showing causality (this happened because of that), so they're a powerful way to show people what happened (the sequence of events) and why (the causes and effects of those events). In a world of hyperlinking and twitter bits, seeing the whole picture, even a small slice, offers "what" and "why," which are critical but often hard to discern.

Make a Case for Media Sharing

The Internet has enabled people to be just-in-time opportunists, getting information when they need it. Employees have that same expectation at work. Short video clips that can be watched on a computer or mobile device are sometimes the best way to deliver that kind of experience fast.

Large organizations have been using audio and video for a long time in marketing and training. What sets the new social media-sharing solutions apart is that they can be fast, broad, and free.

Media sharing, especially video sharing, can provide a captivating way to convey a human voice, rich with emotion and expression, that people trust instinctively more than words on paper or still photos alone. Following are some reasons organizations are turning to rich media.

Eliminate Physical Boundaries

An internal survey at Marathon Oil, with operations spanning three continents, showed that communications from executives weren't delivering the personal impact desired to inspire and inform, and there were no effective ways to gather feedback.[4]

Marathon Oil also faced the challenge of effectively and affordably training dispersed workers on topics ranging from complicated

IT issues to how to properly use a safety mask. For years, Marathon employees accessed documents and presentations over the company network. When Marathon wanted to assure a high level of participation, a trainer went to visit employees on site. This was expensive and resource intensive.

To address this challenge, Marathon originally decided to deliver live video broadcasts over satellite. Several expensive broadcasts later, the company switched to affordable and far-reaching streaming media.

Using an in-house production studio, two dedicated streaming servers, and rich media creation software, Marathon was able to provide live daily streaming webcasts and a library of archived presentations available on demand. The presentations are scalable and can reach all employees at once. Typically 1,200 to 1,400 employees participate in live broadcasts, and as many as 8,000 view on-demand content.

The technology is being used for training in business integrity, hardware operation, legal issues, records retention, wellness advice, health, driver safety, Sarbanes-Oxley compliance, and instruction on software updates. Video brings Marathon executives' personalities and inflections right to employees at their workstations wherever that may be.

Connect with Others

Nearly a decade ago, Nokia began an open discussion forum called Jazz Café where any employee could post questions for the human resources department to answer. The site became one of the most popular online destinations in the company and remains live and active today.

A few years later, the company rolled out wikis for the research and development team and then an online employee directory that allowed people to upload a photo, write a biography, import some data from the ERP system, and link to blogs.

Next Nokia rolled out News Hub, a portal that filters all corporate news. Every employee is able to comment on any news article and rate it, and when there's a particularly controversial piece of news, there are hundreds of posts. Then came Blog Hub, an aggregator of the internal blogosphere, highlighting which blogs are most active, who's commenting, who are the most-read bloggers, and what people are blogging about.

It seemed almost inevitable that the next hub would be for videos. In 2008, the company introduced Video Hub, where any employee who has recorded a video could publish it. It's an aggregator with features for rating, tagging, and commenting on what's been posted. The company has also trained several hundred people to make quality videos and tell stories about Nokia's values in action.

No one moderates the videos, the blogs, or the news. Once posted, they are available to everyone. Fellow employees can report abuse, and if a video is determined to be outside the organization's norms, it is removed, but so far that hasn't been needed. People respect the opportunity to share.

Engage and Influence

Companies have filled their customer-facing websites with rich media, blogs, rating tools, and other interactive features for years. They do that to set themselves apart, stand out, and be memorable in an information-intense world.

Capital One, the credit card monolith, is always pushing the envelope of what consumers should expect from them, so the company wasn't surprised when the rich media experience it helped pioneer influenced its employees' expectations, too.

When employee surveys showed their workplace wasn't as collaborative as it could be, Capital One revamped the corporate intranet to offer more ways to collaborate. It changed the site from a static tool—mostly housing human resources materials such as benefits forms and training schedules—to a lively forum where employees could post, share, and critique ideas, often in video form. My One Place allows anyone with access to the site to contribute and make changes instantaneously.

The need for collaboration and networking was further highlighted following Capital One's acquisition of North Fork Bank of Melville, New York. When the acquisition was final, Capital One's human resources team needed to quickly acclimate North Fork employees to Capital One's culture. The company relied on blogs, podcasts, and informal "Man on the Street" video interviews to help smooth the transition.

Cultivate Culture

A Silicon Valley startup uses video blogging on its intranet for employees and employees' friends and family members to post advice on everything from finding hotels to transforming their cubes into livable habitats. One video is a tour of local eateries, pointing out the specials and clocking how fast you're served.

The videos provide immediate, actionable solutions to common issues facing a young and lean team working around the clock. None of the videos took much time to make, and they were mostly created when someone thought, "I bet my co-workers would benefit from knowing this." The videos also give new employees a sense of the culture and challenges they'll face to show them how to solve problems on their own.

They have also captured their founders talking about how they came up with the idea for the organization and followed people around on their first few days of work as a way to connect people to people and ideas to their originators.

In less than a year, nearly 100 videos were created for fewer than 50 employees. As the startup gains momentum and additional staff, the company plans to incorporate instant video making into its training, human resources, and technical development functions, in the hope of ensuring that the vibrant social culture stays that way, no matter how large the company grows.

Build Trust

As organizations switch to a decentralized or distributed model, transparency from company leaders is a refreshing approach that builds trust and imparts critical insights. When employees are geographically dispersed and "walking the floor" isn't an option, companies use video to reach out in authentic ways.

Video allows leaders to connect more emotionally than a memo or an email, and it's more personal. Videos can be documentary style, or they can be video blogs, town hall meetings, or even company newsreels that cut through corporate spin and deliver information without fluff.

They can be quick talking points, questions and answers, or personal day-in-the-life narratives.

Employees often respond more favorably to a CEO's unscripted comments, filmed by a member of the communication team on a flip-cam, than to a glitzy, professionally shot, heavily scripted, professional video. The more authentic and unfiltered the message, the more credible it generally is.

When two of the world's largest steel manufacturers merged in 2006, Arcelor and Mittal used video to address employees' concerns about the new 320,000-person organization. Short documentaries addressed concerns about layoffs and the merger. The videos became a catalyst for conversations about the changes both inside and outside of the organization, fostering additional support from the market, shareholders, and citizens. Over time, ArcelorMittal launched its own web TV network, loaded with videos and candid conversations with executives and the men and women at the heart of the company sharing their own experiences, challenges, and aspirations.

Establish a Common Identity

ACI Worldwide started as a small company in Omaha, Nebraska, and grew quickly by mergers and acquisitions to 2,200 employees around the globe in 35 countries. Quality standards are taken very seriously; customers in every country on the planet expect software and services to deliver reliable, scalable, and secure payment services every second of every day.

As the company grew, it focused on customers' needs without giving enough thought about infrastructure to integrate facilities, companies, and people around the world—or creating a culture that shared a set of values.

While the company wanted its coders across continents to apply a consistent approach to code development, it also wanted each employee to benefit from the knowledge and experience of other ACI employees. It wanted to drive a profound change, to make ACI functionally and culturally one company.

ACI turned to media sharing through podcasts and videos to capture the knowledge of employees in a way that would allow it to be more easily shared and felt rather than just read. The company showcased the diversity of its people while introducing people's skills and interests, attitudes and perspectives, all aimed at creating products and services everyone could stand behind.

Reinforce Values

RentQuick.com has also turned to media sharing to bring people together and capture what's important. To create fun in bad times, RentQuick .com, a small company that sends high-end audiovisual equipment across the United States and Canada for onsite and offsite meetings, decided to get creative after losing clients during the 2009 recession when meeting planners were laid off and events were cancelled or postponed. Rather than hang heads, lay off staff, or complain, employees kept their spirits high by making videos of funny things they were facing and showing their "make it work" style. They posted them on YouTube and created links to them in their monthly newsletters.

The lighthearted attitude and approach of those at RentQuick.com translated well in short clips. The videos demonstrated that happiness can still exist in tough economic times and that these people are a joy to work with. The videos found new audiences and demonstrated that working with the organization can lead to enjoyable and successful meetings.

Recruit Talent

Prior to being acquired by Accenture, 300-person Gestalt LLC, a software developer in Camden, New Jersey, that serves the defense and energy markets, ran a video contest to spark interest in the company among highly skilled potential recruits.

The contest was open to all employees interested in creating a video and posting it on YouTube. A companywide vote determined the winner, who could opt for an Apple computer or $2,000 in cash. John Moffett won the contest with a 90-second video called *PatrolNET Woes* about a mission through the nearby countryside to "find people."

The video contest encouraged people to create messages that ultimately promoted the company and its culture and climate and was played for the world to see. In a company whose tag line is "value beyond the sum of its parts," this was pushing even its comfort zone. The CEO, Bill Loftus, who admits he was initially nervous about the video contest idea, said "Bigger companies might try to control the message, but I believe a company's true image comes from what people really are, not what spin the marketing department puts on a company." In fact, Gestalt sent a link to the winning video to 16,000 people in its talent database and to various headhunting firms as well.

In the first weekend of sending out the links, the company received 4,000 hits from its candidate database and 750 people reintroduced themselves to the firm. The videos showed the employees' energy and excitement, which positioned the company well in a very competitive market.[5]

> *The video approach shows, rather than tells, prospective recruits that the organization is willing to try new approaches and give employees a public voice to represent the firm.*

Deloitte, as part of its ongoing campaigns to energize the workforce and recruit bright young people, runs an annual International Film Festival, a showcase of three-minute videos posted to YouTube answering the question, "What's Your Deloitte?" Employees can create the videos themselves or work in teams. Everyone from first-year associates to senior partners has made videos, and treatments have included everything from dream sequences to great humor.

The program began as part of an overall strategy for reshaping and refreshing the company culture and specifically encouraging employees to share unfiltered feelings and opinions about what it's like to work at Deloitte. The video approach shows, rather than tells, prospective recruits that the organization is willing to try new approaches and give employees a public voice to represent the firm.

Respond to Critics

As with any new initiative, there will be critics, often well-meaning people who want to keep you from doing dumb things. They have concerns based on their personal experiences or worrisome stories they have heard that they feel compelled to share. Here are the most common objections we hear and ways we believe you can address them.

People Will Post Inappropriate Videos

Giving employees unfettered access to post any videos to the company intranet raises some eyebrows among traditionalists. But concerns about employees posting hurtful, inappropriate, or inflammatory videos have so far been unwarranted at all of the organizations we spoke with—in large part because each post includes the contributor's name.

Social media is generally self-policing. If someone posts something inappropriate, the next person to see it has something to say about it. Media sharing is successful in part because of employee feedback and because so many other people will be watching.

The Value of Media Sharing Can't Be Measured

With any social software, someone usually asks, "How do you measure its value?" Unlike email, for example, media-sharing tools often come with built-in analytics. For example, you may be able to track the following:

- How many visitors watched an entire video before logging off or moving on?
- How many watched only half?
- How many watched only a minute or less?
- How many watched it more than once?

The number and type of questions and comments prompted by each video may provide additional clues to how widely it was viewed and understood. The conversations generated by a video are as valid a measurement of its appeal as the number of times it is viewed, and may even be more valid.

Do you have a communications plan for certain videos that includes a discussion of what viewers learned? Do you provide key messages and questions to help with the discussion? Consider soliciting feedback through a survey to gauge people's understanding and ask whether they found certain videos useful.

In Person Is Always Best

If something needs to be done in person, don't try to accomplish it virtually. But many of the messages we have assumed to be best presented in person are really best done *visually* (seeing the improvisation, hearing the sincerity, getting a sense of a person through his or her body language), and video can make a lasting impression.

Video Isn't for Serious Businesses

Some people associate video with frivolity—the kind of distraction your high school teacher used on a Friday afternoon to control an unruly class. But images, especially when combined into a narrative, are a major component of effective communication. Think of the footage of Neil Armstrong walking on the moon and how that instantly conveyed NASA's mission and purpose.

Videos Are for Fun, Not for Real Knowledge-Transfer

What important lessons have you learned from movies, TV programs, or even from someone telling a story? The power to instruct is inherent in video, too. Create a video of people not communicating well, getting on one another's nerves, or using different communication styles, and you'll quickly see that a visual can teach far more than talking when something goes wrong.

Recommendations

Get started with a media-sharing plan by considering what people in your organization and the ecosystem of business partners, contractors, and possibly even customers would benefit from seeing and hearing.

Start Where You Are

When employee-generated audio and video can be posted on content platforms the company already has, such as IBM Lotus Quickr, Sharepoint ECM, Cisco Show and Share, or Google Business Services, start-up costs will be relatively low and IT will already be versed in some of what you're trying to do. If your organization doesn't already use a content management system, consider beginning by creating a YouTube channel and posting a few publicly sharable videos to get the hang of it. Then look at some of the emerging media-sharing platforms to see which one fits your needs.

Clarify Your Intentions and Your Mix

Your corporate technology culture, the application literacy of your workforce, and the number of people who have access to recording devices—be it smartphones, flip cameras, digital audio recorders, or a growing number of media capture devices—will determine how many people will be interested in contributing to and consuming your media collection. Add executive and training videos to that, and you have a critical mass. It's unlikely, at least at first, that every employee will create and upload videos, but even when a small number of creators is responsible for the bulk of the content, a much larger number of people will critique it, and an even larger number will benefit.

Promote the Best Examples of Employee-Generated Video

When employees can comment on, share, and embed the best clips in their own emails, blog posts, wikis, and team sites, the most effective material will gain value. You can also jumpstart viral adoption by giving certain clips prominence around the organization. Consider asking for volunteers willing to spend off hours finding the best videos on the internal site and rating them to give them more exposure.

Pick Easy-to-Use Technologies

Look for technology where, once employees touch it, they understand it because they are familiar with the Internet; because they have used Facebook, MySpace, or Twitter; or because they have already made a personal investment in the learning curve and can immediately begin to use the tools, greatly speeding up adoption.

Give Executives a Direct Link with Employees

Turn executives' messages into short video or audio streams. Post them on the Intranet, web portal, or online community; pipe them to screens in the entryway; and offer the videos to customers who want to hear the CEO's perspective.

Celebrate Wins, Train Salespeople, and Showcase Team Spirit

When the sales team has a big win or the development team passes an important milestone, someone inevitably captures the celebration through video and shares it far and wide. At large meetings, encourage people throughout the event to use flipcams to videotape almost everything. Then show onstage how the event met the expectations and objectives set out at the beginning. This rallies the troops; shares lessons from those practicing their sales pitches, such as presenters in sessions talking about an important upcoming product release; and showcases a group of people deeply interested in helping their organization succeed.

Use Video to Communicate Privately with Business Partners

Instead of posting that confidential clip on YouTube, post it safely on a protected extranet site and invite your partners to view and comment on it. This makes video a great tool for agencies to share with advertisers, for insurance companies to train independent agents, or for a manufacturer to show problems to suppliers.

Capture Corporate Knowledge Through Expert Interviews

As some of the longtime gurus of a company head toward retirement, solving big problems and focusing on what they do best, newer employees have little opportunity to learn from them. When a senior developer gives notice, have a new member of the communications team trail him or her for a week, discovering everything he or she does, asking questions, and capturing for others to learn from in the years ahead. Through interviews or even simply capturing them in action, media sharing can transform people's experiences, stories, and living examples into easily consumable knowledge before it walks out the door.

If you do something very simple, such as implement a system in which your people know where to go to get the information they need to get their jobs done, you can save people a couple of minutes a day. You generate savings when your people don't need to search through their email because they can go to a community and search easily through media clips on topics that pertain to them. Right there they also find news about the organization and tips from their teammates, which is more time saved. You can calculate that a couple of minutes per person per day adds up to 45 minutes per employee per month. That equals nine hours per year. These are very conservative estimates of the time saved. That little calculation does not even include the benefits you can realize from the improved quality and customer service. It's just that simple.

Microsharing for a Healthy Culture

"Productive people, busy people, busier and more productive than you can imagine people feel better connected and in touch with the ideas around them than ever before because of microsharing. This aggregation of thoughts is easy to assimilate, without adding more data load on them, and without sacrificing their attention."

—Montgomery Flinsch
Senior Technical Architect, Mayo Clinic

◆ ◆ ◆

Humans have conveyed short messages, long with meaning, for as long as 40,000 years. Smoke signals have traversed the airways. Expressive quips filled the Seinfeld show. At all stages and ages, we move forward in small bursts of communication. Some people just don't notice how much can be conveyed when just a little is said.

Microsharing is the class of social software tools that enables people to update one another with short bursts of text, links, and multimedia either through standalone applications or as part of larger online communities or social networks.

Messages sent this way usually can't exceed 140 characters. This restriction isn't arbitrary. One hundred and sixty characters is the total that mobile devices (SMS) can accept; 140 characters for the message and the remaining 20 for the bits of data necessary for identifying the source of the information. Within these 140 characters, people can ask questions, post feedback, highlight news stories, and link to items on the Internet.

Microsharing emerges from a trend to make digital content smaller and faster to spread. It is eclipsing email (too slow) and texting (too restricted an audience). Microbursts of information are easy to read and write, there is nothing to delete, you can communicate one to one or one to many, and replies are optional.

Microsharing doesn't require any special technical knowledge to use or any complex technology to deploy. The software can route messages to people's desktops, laptops, and devices already in pockets and purses without depending on local email servers or phone trees. These utilities can quickly convey text messages or images to an extended enterprise, a decentralized workforce, a dispersed campus, a community of practice, a small group of friends, or just one person who needs to know.

> *Microsharing is a powerful way to connect people for personal, professional, or corporate benefit.*

The best-known microsharing software, at the time of writing this book, is Twitter. The actor Ashton Kutcher was the first to acquire a million followers on Twitter (beating out rival CNN Breaking News for the honor). Barack Obama's campaign for president made wide use of Twitter to reach voters. And millions of ordinary people use it every day to send and receive very short messages, amplifying voices, netting people-picked answers fast, facilitating listening, and enabling a natural approach to being aware of the community around them.

Microsharing is a powerful way to connect people for personal, professional, or corporate benefit. With enterprise-focused Twitter-like tools such as Socialcast, Socialtext Signals, Cubetree, and Yammer, designed specifically for private use, organizations can now bring microsharing capabilities in house. Because they operate behind the firewall, these tools help protect confidential information and can link back to other enterprise systems.

The Mayo Clinic experience with microsharing illustrates the tool's power. When you leave the Mayo Clinic you may not be cured, but you will know what's wrong and you will feel capable of making the decisions ahead of you. That's enormous comfort for the half a million people who pass through one of Mayo's three campuses each year. For those who have suffered with chronic illness or a medical matter their local doctor knew little about, their trip to Mayo has changed them, providing answers, insights, and a better quality of life. In many cases, it gives them their lives back.

The first and largest integrated not-for-profit medical practice in the world, the Mayo Clinic employs more than 57,000 physicians, scientists, researchers, allied health professionals, and residents. The world-class staff, deeply entrenched in labor-intensive intellectual work, aim to create a culture of collaborative care—with social media, a new and vital resource.

Consider, for example, a Mayo radiologist who was sitting alone in a darkened room looking at x-rays. He saw something he'd never seen before and asked himself, "What the heck is *that*?" A few minutes later, he used Mayo's internal microsharing network, asking the question, "How can we use [microsharing] clinically?" Also referred to as microblogging, social messaging, and micromessaging, this network carries very small Twitter-like messages, using systems specifically designed for use *within* organizations. His question led to a two-week conversation online about what using microsharing clinically might mean. Out of that dialogue, three people, the radiologist, a physician, and a technical program manager, who had never crossed paths before, agreed to do something about this question.

They could see their colleagues were curious and interested in the topic of microsharing in a shared clinical environment to provide just-in-time knowledge support for an unusual diagnosis. The wisdom of crowds told them the topic was worth taking on.

They agreed to write a proposal and contemplated how they should do it. The project manager suggested two weeks of meetings. The radiologist and physician suggested they should send ideas across the microsharing system until they figured out what they wanted, until the ideas were better formed, and only then move their primary collaboration space to an internal wiki. That's what they did. They challenged themselves to hold no face-to-face meetings and exchange no email. They met that challenge, wrote the proposal to study how to do microsharing well clinically, got funded to run the project, and only met in person for the first time when they received the funding. Out of their microsharing experiment, they gained tangible examples and practice with the tools and produced enduring tangible work: the conversation they had with one another and others chiming in and the wiki. They left behind no voicemails, texts, file attachments—no digital clutter. And they did this all in about three weeks, super fast by most medical community standards. The process wasn't dramatically different than if the same people worked well together in a small office every day. A new idea was identified and moved into productive work. A team was formed, with synchronous time coordination. When most people don't work side by side, how do you find the right people, put them together, and form a cohesive team to do productive work without flying everyone to Atlanta once a week or adjusting everyone's schedule so they can meet together down the hall?

Monty Flinsch, who has led technical initiatives at Mayo's central campus in Rochester, Minnesota, for more than a decade, sees the endless potential of microsharing to establish and support relationships between people and departments. He doesn't see these tools used to develop knowledge. He sees microsharing as a critical component for Mayo clinicians to make vital connections.[1]

A physical scientist by training, Flinsch likens microsharing to cloud seeding, the distribution of silver iodine that changes the energy in clouds and leads to rain. When people ask a question or post a link to a resource across Mayo's internal microsharing tools, their open sharing creates a place where ideas get crystallized. Ideas ignite more sharing and then normal human relationships take off. People go to lunch, talk on the phone, or invite each other to see something they are working on.

Because this happens more frequently and sooner than if someone had to make introductions, or they read about the challenge on a piece of paper near the elevator, people at Mayo are making more substantial contacts. They spark off of one another's ideas. Connecting again online or in person reinvigorates the process and brings new energy to their communications. For busy people who need to find ways to manage their attention stream, microsharing seems just little enough to not seem like a burden. It's akin to writing a paper or a blog without the time commitment. It's sufficiently lightweight to fit into the spaces between the critical work people do.

Physicians at Mayo, like people in many professions, face a huge number of system alerts begging for their attention. Microsharing can become their unified activity stream, which they can look at through the corner of an eye and receive alerts and gain an ambient awareness of conversations going on. Rather than being bombarded with notices that blood work is complete, a room is ready, or a package has arrived, this unified stream is there when they are ready to review it.

Although some people believe that microsharing adds to chaos and perceive it as just more noise, others find threads of relevance in their first few experiences. They use it as a digest, checking in once in a while and getting an idea where the institution is on a topic, what's up. One more blip isn't distracting; they view the microsharing stream when they have time. They can engage when appropriate.

> *For busy people who need to find ways to manage their attention stream, microsharing seems just little enough to not seem like a burden. It's akin to writing a paper or a blog without the time commitment. It's sufficiently lightweight to fit into the spaces between the critical work people do.*

Ideas get tossed out, and some fall to the bottom of the pile (when there isn't a reply or conversation). Others stick, and engagement ensues. Messages touch a nerve or mix with threads that keep popping up, forming a pulse of the institution. When there's internal rumbling, you can sense it across the stream. Ideas are refined in the space, issues get aired, and people feel connected to one another and to the vibe of the organization.

Mayo also uses microsharing and other social media tools to reach out beyond its campuses, connecting with and educating people about

Mayo Clinic practices. The organization engages with three key audiences: the public with health-related questions and concerns, prospective patients, and the medical and research communities.

The technology chosen for this communication gives both Mayo employees and the larger community a sense of personal connectedness to the organization and its people and a sustained commitment to leading-edge use of technologies that always put people first.

In 2009, Mayo Clinic held a conference called "Transform," run by its center for innovation. The 400 participants included the inventor of Swiffer at Procter & Gamble and people from IDEO, GE, IBM, MIT Media Lab, Massachusetts General Hospital, and the Darden School of Business. It was a gathering of large enterprise innovators, specifically designed to spark interaction among leading-edge thinkers and promote conversation about innovation at Mayo itself.

Run six months after the launch of its microsharing network pilot, the organization saw a 50 percent increase in the number of people sharing online. Inside the organization, people who were not at the event but were watching it unfold online introduced new thoughts, shared ideas, and chronicled highlights as if they were at the conference.

Virtual participants across the microsharing stream appointed themselves as connectors and advocates, spreading ideas out several nodes to all corners of the organization. People wouldn't have had that special feeling of "I got to participate in something amazing" if it weren't for microsharing. It extended creative thinking to the whole organization without the cost and logistical headaches of a 50,000-person seminar.

Suffering from chronic wrist pain, Erin Turner, an account supervisor at a health-focused public relations agency, noticed a tweet from @MayoClinic about a Twitter chat with a prestigious hand surgeon about wrist pain. Thinking this could be her opportunity for some answers, Turner followed the provided link to a page on the Mayo website with a link to a *USA Today* article about a different type of ligament tear; illustrations and video about the condition; a patient testimonial video; a podcast; a list of doctors trained in diagnosing and treating this condition; video of Dr. Richard Berger, the surgeon, explaining his discovery and the typical treatment course; and even a journal article about the condition.

Over the course of an hour-long chat, Turner was able to tell Dr. Berger about the pain she experienced and the options she had been provided. He thought more was going on with her wrist than previous diagnoses had shown. For the first time in a long time, she felt hope for a future without chronic pain. She gathered all her medical information and made an appointment with Berger at the Mayo Clinic.

Less than 24 hours after her appointment, she not only had a new diagnosis, she also had surgery to correct the problem. She had a brighter future that, without Twitter and people in the medical community willing to experiment with new communications tools, might not exist.[2]

Microsharing holds great promise for the scientific process because it allows scientists even in unrelated fields to discuss their thorniest problems with each other in ways that don't intrude too much into their lives.

Monty Flinsch says, "These technologies create energy that is self-sustaining. Microsharing provides a simple way for people to connect, set ideas on fire, and make ideas rain."

Burst Forward

Enterprise microsharing can help address a dueling dilemma for organizations needing to move knowledge where people need it now and keeping information from leaking out of the organization. Most microsharing tools allow message writers to control how messages are shared and who sees them. They also allow message receivers to keep track of ("follow") the people writing them.

When you read a timeline from the list of followers that you have chosen personally, you have total control. Therefore, if the tweets you are reading are 40 percent pointless babble, you can easily fix this by not following them anymore.

Although some organizations formally ban these tools, doing so leaves them out of an important loop encompassing customers, partner networks, and even families. As the boundaries between personal and work life dissolve, organizations see more productivity and loyalty from people who once dreaded leaving their private lives in the parking lot as they walked through the door to work. Microsharing, the technological equivalent of water-cooler chat, offers clues to those around us, leading us to know, trust, and help one another. It's in the little learning moments that you recall that Jeff isn't just a guy in product development, but a parent with a daughter about the same age as your son. People tell us they have learned more about their co-workers and customers from their micro-messages and social media profiles than they have from working together for years.

Aaron Silvers, community manager for Advanced Distributed Learning (ADL), describes social networking as an act of sharing actions. He began using Twitter to connect with peers and industry leaders who could help solve his toughest on-the-job challenges. He was working at the industrial supply company Grainger and saw that microsharing could add value to Grainger's education initiatives and provide people across the organization new ways to engage. Says Silvers, "Once Twitter made sense to me, I saw its potential as a tool to connect employees to each other. Maybe not Twitter itself, but at least a tool like it. Something that could be secure yet accessible could kick start social networking in an organization."[3]

Then a senior executive at Grainger saw the media attention over Twitter and signed up for the grassroots enterprise microsharing community Silvers helped set up. Two hours later, the executive posted to his company blog that he had created an internal microsharing account and that he'd begun using it to talk with employees. By 8:00 a.m. the following morning, the system had 306 users. Within a few weeks, more than a thousand people had joined in.

A year later, more than 3,000 people were microsharing back and forth, many using the system for far more than learning what's on the leaders' minds. People shared stories and observations, what they'd learned with customers, and how they could improve their work. Microsharing hasn't changed the company's culture dramatically. Silvers maintains that culture change was not the explicit goal; learning was. People at all levels share what they're working on and have conversations on topics they feel passionate about. This gives everyone an opportunity to learn from those who are willing to share their expertise.

Too frequently organizational knowledge sharing mirrors the news-cycle society around us, in which we share the highs and lows, ignoring the ordinary stuff in the middle. It's in that middle ground that people make sense of the work going on around them, understand how to help fulfill the company vision, and know where to turn to find help.

These slender messages are interstitial; they lie in and fill the seams of organizations. Learning often entails asking people how to do things. The trouble is we customarily ask the person closest to us rather than someone known to have the right answer. Microsharing helps us reach the right people without even knowing who they are. You can also enlist help en masse by asking large groups of people to focus on the same issue for a short burst of time to find a creative solution quickly.

> *Too frequently organizational knowledge sharing mirrors the news-cycle society around us, in which we share the highs and lows, ignoring the ordinary stuff in the middle. It's in that middle ground that people make sense of the work going on around them, understand how to help fulfill the company vision, and know where to turn to find help.*

The threads help us collectively construct understanding, foster new connections, and grow existing bonds, making for more agile perspectives, tighter teams, and resilient morale.

These tools work similarly to how we converse while passing one another in the hallway, representing a live ecosystem that shifts from moment to moment, where it is easier, faster, and more effective for us to brain dump as events happen.

Dave Wilkins, vice president of product marketing at Learn.com says, "Microsharing is not for sharing the minutiae of my day. I use it to share the insights and sources that shape my professional thinking and to connect my professional dots."[4]

Edu-Tweet

The ability to send and receive updates is a key feature of microsharing. Update boxes usually have a phrase that prompts you to answer a question. Twitter's has been, "What Are You Doing?" and "What's Happening?" Yammer and Socialtext Signals ask, "What Are You Working On?" Socialcast says, "Share something with _____" and the blank is a dropdown of your groups and streams. Cubetree asks, "What's on your mind?" And some systems don't have prompt questions at all, but provide a freeform space where you compose your message.

Most people don't answer those precise questions. Instead they ask and answer questions relevant to their own situations. Or they answer an unspoken question such as, "What has your attention?" "Can you assist me?" or "What did you learn today?" Answering these questions encourages you to reflect on what's occurring around you and to consider what's on your mind.

In general, updates fall into three types: the current status of what you are doing, questions about what others are doing and how they might help you, and general information that many might need quickly.

Here are some examples.

I. Questions from You to Others

"Can You Help Me?"

This type of question has many variants, which all involve seeking something from other people—advice, feedback, recommendations, answers, and so on.

New York Times writer David Pogue likes to share an example that won him over to Twitter, which he used to think of as an ego-massaging, social-networking time drain. "Who on earth has the bandwidth to keep interrupting their work to visit a website and type in, 'I'm now having lunch' and to read the same trivia from a hundred other people?" He didn't get it, and he didn't think he wanted to get it.[5]

Then his eyes opened. He was one of 12 judges for a MacArthur grant. As the jury looked over one particular application, someone asked, "Hasn't this project been tried before?" Everyone looked blank. Then the guy sitting next to Pogue posed the question to his followers on Twitter. Within 30 seconds, two people replied that it had been done before and provided links.

They harnessed the power of a large group of people—a process often referred to as "crowdsourcing"—in real time. No email, chat, web page, phone call, or FedEx package could have achieved the same thing. People who use microsharing to get expert advice on the fly, even those with fairly small groups of people who have opted to receive their tweets (followers), can attest to the fact that it usually returns results immediately.

Ben Betts, operations director for HT2 Ltd., a UK-based e-learning and organization development company, used one of his first Twitter updates to ask about the Adobe Flash player. Much to his surprise and delight, someone from Adobe responded within moments.[6]

Companies including JetBlue, Comcast, Wellpoint, and The Home Depot use Twitter for instant customer support. Associates who are stumped for answers to customers' questions put out a request through their internal microsharing systems for help from their colleagues, and the answers come streaming back.

> *Companies including JetBlue, Comcast, Wellpoint, and The Home Depot use Twitter for instant customer support. Associates who are stumped for answers to customers' questions put out a request through their internal microsharing systems for help from their colleagues, and the answers come streaming back.*

"What Are You Learning?"

You're attending a conference. Minutes into a session, you notice people in the audience tapping furiously on their smartphones and reading incoming messages. Some of them get up and leave the room, while another bunch trickles in.

Chances are they're tweeting about the session, asking questions, and getting the scoop on sessions their friends are attending that might be more relevant than the one they're in. This kind of instant learning has become the subtext of many conferences.

Gary Hegenbart, senior training developer at Calix, said of one conference, "The Twitter activity was overwhelming. In every session I attended there were people tweeting about it. Although it was sometimes hard to pay attention and tweet at the same time, we wanted to share small nuggets of learning. I got real-time reports—positive and nega-tive—on the sessions I missed, and I benefited from others sharing the highlights of those sessions."[7]

"How Can I Excel Here?"

This is a common question from new employees. Independently or using systems set up by their employers, new hires find out with one click who has influence, what practices have been vetted, and how they can get ahead quickly. Because these tools record exchanges, it's possible to learn how a concept, plan, or project evolved in the company, even if you didn't participate in the original process.

Faith LeGendre, senior global consultant for customer advocacy in Cisco's collaboration software group, used microsharing to help her thrive in Cisco's culture. When she was a new employee, working away from headquarters, she sought a seasoned employee to mentor her. Within sec-onds of making her request on Cisco's internal microsharing system, a woman in a completely different area responded. They have shared and learned together ever since.

In other companies, LeGendre had spent hours searching through intranets and distant servers to learn about her employer, her role, and how things really worked. Now, by asking others for guidance via microsharing, she not only receives the exact information she needs, but it often comes with extra insights. For example, someone might respond, "Don't forget 2 fill out section C way at bottom or it will get rejected in the automatic system." She constantly learns from colleagues around the globe and saves time while increasing her productivity and accuracy.[8]

"How Does This Work?"

This is a question you will often see when people are trying to figure out how to do something new and they're pretty sure someone else has already tried it. They're tapping into that wisdom of crowds that so impressed David Pogue.

Manish Mohan in Chennai, India, and Tom Stone in Rochester, New York, use an internal microsharing system at Element K to share links, seek insights from their colleagues, and test a pilot of an internal microsharing system across their entire organization, including their sister company Cognitive Arts and their parent company, NIIT, based in Delhi.

The benefits of microsharing became evident to Mohan early on when he asked his followers about a function in Lotus Notes. It happened to be a question that many others were also curious about, and Stone knew the answer. If Mohan had asked his question by email, his chances of getting an answer would have been low unless he sent the message to a big list. It was more efficient for him to cast his question across microsharing where people tune in with the expectation of engaging in conversation. It was also better for his colleagues because they saw his question and Stone's response, which they wouldn't have seen over email.[9]

"How Am I Doing?"

Pragmatic people want feedback on their performance in real time and can now get it faster than ever before. Instead of waiting months for a formal review from their manager, people have begun to ask others, using microsharing tools and other social software, to help them learn how to improve right away.

Although most microsharing tools were not designed for performance feedback, many people use them that way. "What do you think of this article I wrote? See the link here . . ." or "Was it dumb to attempt running the compiler before I. . . ." Likewise, at conferences, attendees tweet feedback to presenters and share their reviews of sessions with their online networks, not just the people at the event.

Conference speakers and educators have begun to use microsharing to create and sustain relationships and dialogue around sessions and classes. Jane Hart, social learning consultant and founder of the Centre for Learning and Performance Technologies in Wiltshire, England, says,

> *Companies are also using updating tools to make regular checks on what people are learning and how they are progressing toward their objectives. Employees microshare their goals with a group of people selected to provide input. Sending regular updates encourages people to reflect on what they're doing and learning and makes them mindful of sharing with people they work with or serve.*

"As an instructor, you can have immediate feedback on the relevance of your class. It turns training into a more participatory activity."[10]

Companies are also using updating tools to make regular checks on what people are learning and how they are progressing toward their objectives. Employees microshare their goals with a group of people selected to provide input. Sending regular updates encourages people to reflect on what they're doing and learning and makes them mindful of sharing with people they work with or serve.

Niche microsharing tools such as Rypple, Coworkers.com, and en.dorse. me are specifically for those times when employees want to go to trusted friends and advisors to get what they consider real feedback. These tools make it quick and easy to collect input from the bottom up and from peers.

"Which People Should I Know?"

People often use microsharing networks to find subject matter experts, grow their professional networks, or maximize a conference experience.

Michelle Lentz, an independent trainer and professional blogger, began using Twitter to get to know other training professionals.[11] Within months, she was posting regular updates about her work, getting help from experts, and attracting followers of her own. She found it expanded her network tenfold. At conferences, she began to hear a recurring theme from people she met, "I follow you on Twitter." Instant friendship.

She tells her students that they must go out and find the right people on Twitter (or their internal microsharing sites). Do you want to know more about your brand? Monitor it through Twitter. A simple Twitter search, or use of sites such as Twellow, can open up doors for you. Do you want to know more about a hobby? Do a search on that hobby and follow the people discussing it.

Such microsharing-based encounters really can create instantaneous camaraderie based on similar interests and a history of online conversations. Microsharing accelerates the conversation because if you just met someone you follow or who follows you, then you already know a lot about the person. You've experienced ambient awareness. It feels like a reunion and conversation flows freely.

Lentz landed a new part-time job for a technology blog after she started following on Twitter the author of several of her favorite social media marketing books, Brian Solis. He tweeted that he was looking for someone he could pay to write occasional technology and gadget posts. She replied via Twitter, having never spoken to him before, and within 24 hours she had a fantastic and fun new writing job and had connected over the phone with one of her favorite authors. Instant opportunity.

Microsharing encourages you to share and be involved, even if it's only 140 characters at a time. The sense of community and wanting to give back to the community can be palpable because now there are people there you know, trust, and want to learn with.

II. Updates About You to Others

"Here's What I'm Doing"

Many people at work use microsharing updates to let others know what they are working on, reading, and thinking about. This is not self-centered boasting. By sharing their interests, people plant seeds that might lead to a connection with someone who could reveal new insights, point to new resources, help with a project, or simply confirm that you're not the only person in your network interested in Egyptian art or complexity theory.

"Here's What Our Organization Is Doing"

Although many such updates from companies are a form of marketing, they also remind people what's coming up that they should know about, learning opportunities they might want to explore, or trends in an industry.

A growing number of organizations use Twitter to foster communication among employees and customers. Southwest Airlines tweets first-time customers with the message, "Hope you enjoyed your first-ever Southwest flight! Can't wait to see you onboard again." Mayo Clinic uses its Twitter account to share integrated health care practices, publicize medical news, and answer health-related questions.

Gina Minks, senior social media program manager at EMC, uses its internal microsharing network for internal marketing messages such as, "Please ask your customers to participate in the global survey on managing information and storage. Click here for details." And, "Wondering about Cloud Computing? Check out the Cloud Computing Fundamentals eLearning, free till March 31."[12]

"What Are You Working On?"

Instead of asking for periodic progress reports, Claudia Miro, when she led client services at a midsize coaching and consulting firm, used microsharing and other social media tools to keep tabs on her virtual workforce spread throughout North America. They relied on short exchanges to share, collaborate, and communicate about the work they were doing with clients. It was not unusual for a consultant to get a quick microburst from Miro, broadcast to all the consultants, asking for a report on who they met, how much time they spent, and what were the outcomes. The organization began using social tools as an internal document repository for operations; yet over time, it grew to become a dynamic communications tool across their internal and external partners. By capturing learning in the moment, the organization could quickly leverage the collective knowledge of its consultants and provide more value and collective intelligence, to the organizations it served.[13]

"Where Are You Heading?"

Bob Picciano, general manager of IBM Software Sales, uses microsharing tools to narrate part of his work and share his whereabouts with various teams. When he posted on IBM's internal microsharing tool that he was heading to a town where he hadn't been before for an important customer meeting, within a few minutes an IBM sales rep asked if Picciano might have time to meet with another customer in the same city. Picciano met with both customers that day, helped close a sale he didn't even know about when he woke up that morning, and established a new and now long-standing relationship with another part of his organization.[14]

III: Information Many People Need Now

"What Do People Need to Know Right Now?"

Companies have operational updates that need to reach people at certain times to coordinate the system that is an organization. There's information each person in an organizational ecosystem needs to help that enterprise succeed. This information can be broadcast ("Amazing guest speaking in the auditorium on Friday afternoon") or narrowcast to specific groups ("Our meeting has moved to the fourth floor conference room").

Although people—for instance someone in human resources, accounting, legal, or the front desk—generate most broadcast messages, they can also be automated to inform people at critical times. An order-processing system can kick out events and exceptions. A benefits system can signal coverage changes and enrollment deadlines. A learning management system can prompt people to renew certifications or announce a new online course.

Shel Israel, author of *Twitterville* and co-author of *Naked Conversations*, tells of the San Diego Metro Transit System, one of many public transit systems using Twitter to give passengers real-time information about delays, snags, and changes. Newcastle [UK] City Council's secretary Alistair Smith tweets school closings with greater currency than the BBC provides.[15]

Microsharing systems offer unified access to information relevant to each of us, one at a time and all at the same time.

Twitter Lingo

Tweet: Twitter updates. You post tweets. You are tweeting. You have tweeted.

@username: Your unique identifier on Twitter (for example, @marciamarcia and @tonybingham). Can also list an organization, for example, @astd or @berrettkoehler. People with Twitter accounts can also be reached on http://twitter.com/username.

Following: People with Twitter accounts whose tweets you choose to follow.

Followers: People with Twitter accounts who have chosen to follow you.

Retweet (RT): Repeat a post you find interesting or useful that was originally posted by someone else on Twitter.

Direct message (DM): A Twitter function that allows you to contact privately someone who follows you by prefacing your tweet with the letter D and then his or her userid.

Reply (@): The way to direct a tweet to an individual twitter account, which can be seen by anyone who follows that person.

Hashtag (#): Words or acronyms used in a tweet and preceded by a # to help people track topics, communities, live events, or breaking news.

Favorites: A way to recognize certain tweets as your best loved.

Lists: A way to create a grouping of people on Twitter whose messages you want to see in a stream. You can make public lists that others can subscribe to and private lists for your sole use.

Stream: A list of messages generated by the people you follow.

Backchannel: A stream of tweets, sometimes using a shared hashtag, for a particular conference, presentation, or event.

Tweetup: A gathering of people who come together in person after first connecting via Twitter.

Shortener: Tools that shrink a web address so it takes up fewer characters.

"Let Me Help You Learn"

A few years ago it would have been hard to imagine teaching anything 140 characters at a time. But as training events and courses give way to more immediate forms of instruction, microsharing plays a role in training. Informal information exchanges in real time supplement structured learning events.

Kelly Forrister, vice president of interactive learning at The David Allen Company, has been using Twitter to lead classes on lessons from Allen's book *Getting Things Done*. She selected two modules, GTD Weekly Review and Mind Sweep, because they have somewhat set models and structures. She created a special Twitter account and at specific dates and times, she pushes content out—140 characters at a time—to people who follow that account. They take action based on the tweet and ask her questions along the way through @replies.

Nearly 1,500 people follow the account from around the globe. Feedback floods in about its value. Many people especially like having someone guide them through a process they don't have the discipline or motivation to go through on their own. Forrister doesn't consider this a replacement for instructor-led or e-learning courses but rather a compelling way to lead people and engage with them virtually.[16]

> *Microsharing gives students a way to toss insights and questions to other students without taking time away from the instructor. Microsharing can provide links to articles, webinars, and other resources. It can also be used to reinforce and sustain learning.*

Microsharing gives students a way to toss insights and questions to other students without taking time away from the instructor. Microsharing can provide links to articles, webinars, and other resources. It can also be used to reinforce and sustain learning. Educators can post tips of the day, answers to questions from students, writing assignments, and other prompts and reminders about key points to keep learning going. It's an easy way to stimulate conversation among a group before, during, and after any sort of event. Anyone in the group can share his or her points of view and familiar practices.

Respond to Critics

Possibly more than any other social media tool, microsharing seems frivolous to people who have never tried it; even some who have tried it don't see its usefulness. To encourage people to use it long enough to find value, you may need to talk with them about it and show them specifically how to get past first impressions. Here are the most common objections we hear and ways we believe you can address them.

I Have Too Much to Say

At first it may take several posts to convey your meaning, though in time you'll discover more precise ways to write. Amid shrinking attention spans and increasing distractions, we all need skills to craft clear and concise messages. Once mastered, you can apply this sharpness to other tasks: answering questions, writing crisp instructions, or making a case for launching something new. Just because you can explain more doesn't mean you should. Be brief, even if writing succinctly takes time.

Use your 140 characters for interesting statistics, personal analysis, or as a launch pad to longer and more nuanced content on your blog, comments you've posted elsewhere, or your online community profile. Link people directly to what you see and tell them why you care.

I Don't Have Time

If you think, "I can't tweet. I have real work to do," ask yourself this question: In the two minutes between a phone call and a meeting, could you share what you learned on the call and seek insight for the meeting? What about while waiting for a webinar to start or, if you carry a smartphone, in line at the grocery store or the post office? Turn your open minutes into learning moments.

When you connect through microsharing with people who share your professional and personal interests, you may also save time. They'll point you to vetted materials in less time than it would take you to scan through Google results or an RSS feed. Your network distributes useful information to you wherever you are and on your own terms.

I Can't Participate Because My Company Blocks Its Use

Consider signing up for a personal Twitter account from home so that when your company loosens restrictions, you'll have experience with the tools. This will happen. Each day more organizations are amending their strict policies as they realize employees have smartphones in their pockets and a younger, more digitally minded generation expects the workplace to support online engagement.

Until then or in addition, with the emergence of microsharing tools for the enterprise, even the most security-conscious organizations can bring these capabilities in house. Some tools even offer the safety of working behind a firewall to protect discussions about confidential, proprietary, or personally identifiable information. You can find more information about these tools on The New Social Learning website (http://thenewsociallearning.com).

It's Only for Young People with Time on Their Hands

CEOs and industry leaders of all ages are beginning to use microsharing to open dialogues within their organizations, throughout enterprises, and with potential customers. By responding to a few words and a question mark, people provide expert testimony, gut-level hunches, and a field view that organizations might never capture otherwise.

Are senior leaders telling their microsharing followers what they had for lunch? Probably not. Are they distributing observations while waiting for a delayed flight? Maybe. Do they believe microsharing offers business value? Certainly.

Dan Cathy, COO of Chick-fil-A, told us in an interview that he and the company are enthusiastic users of microsharing tools. "We see it as leveraging influence. . . . The reason I'm on Facebook is not because I need something else to do with my time. Through my activity on Twitter, more people will know that I'm practicing what I preach."[17]

Bill Ives, vice president of marketing at Darwin Ecosystems and a 20-year veteran of the enterprise software industry points out, "These tools allow me to connect with smart people regardless of age or tech-savvy. They honor my busy schedule and let me focus on my business."[18]

It's Overwhelming

Microsharing is a serendipity engine. Rather than expecting yourself to keep up with every message, focus on what's before you when you check in and rely on direct messages, replies, and retweets to learn who is ready to engage.

Short messages allow you to approach updates with a newspaper headline mindset, scanning assorted posts quickly, ignoring the uninteresting, and focusing on those that captivate you. This means you can easily process a message stream and then turn your attention back to other tasks.

Answers Are Hit or Miss

Sometimes someone new to microsharing posts a question and no one replies. That's often because they don't have many followers accustomed to replying. Or maybe the question isn't worded in a way that makes it clear you're asking for a response. Or people may be ignoring your question because they don't know you.

Microsharing can be compared to a large party filled with people you don't know. If you huddle near the punch bowl and hors d'oeuvres, you're not likely to have many conversations. At first, you might wonder why you came. Early posts often include phrases such as, "Trying to figure this out," and "Why am I here?" Then you begin listening in on other people's conversations, looking for a good time to speak up. Once others notice you, they may involve you in the conversation, and you may see a good opening to ask a question. At that point, the likelihood of a reply is far higher than when you first showed up.

Seek out people who share your interests and who are most likely to have answers to the types of question you ask. After you enter the fray, if you still aren't getting answers, direct a question to someone you'd especially like to hear from, and make it clear you'd welcome responses from others as well. Rather than, "Do you know which Nikon lenses work with a full-frame sensor camera?"—which can be interpreted as a yes-no quiz instead of a question—try "Anyone know if the Nikon AF-S VR 24-120 lens works with the D700? Welcome your insights."

I Don't Know How to Use It

Twitter tutorials are everywhere. A quick search will yield blogs, online courses, in-person workshops, books, and video instruction on YouTube. Really, all you need to do is create an account, connect to several people mentioned in this book, think about what's holding your attention, and tell us a little about what you've learned.

When the people you follow round out their contributions with something educational, learning will zing wild and flow free. Twitter founder Jack Dorsey says, "Twitter is for connecting people through real-time updates that spark conversation and expose trends."[19] We believe that enterprise microsharing may be bigger than that. Just as blogs give us all a free, personal printing press on the Internet, microsharing provides an instant, real-time connection to people we want to learn from.

We challenge everyone who reads this to try edu-twittering for a week. Tell us through the @NewSocialLearn account on Twitter that you're on board. We'll learn together what happens.

Recommendations

Whether you are interested in using Twitter or an internal microsharing platform, the steps for getting started are fairly similar. The main difference is where you sign up or sign in.

Sign Up

To create a Twitter account, go to http://twitter.com. If your organization already has a relationship with an enterprise microsharing vendor (or microsharing is a feature in another social medium such as an online community), you'll go to the entrance to that site to sign up there. If your organization hasn't begun working with an internal tool, you can find a list of providers on The New Social Learning website (http://thenewsocial learning.com), which tells you a little bit about the differences and benefits of each. Basically, you'll go to the provider's website and supply a bit of information about your organization to create the account and then sign up. Once you create a username and password, you will be asked for additional information such as a basic biography, a photo, and a link to where people can learn more about you. Don't wait to add those details—especially a photo—because these are the touches of someone interested in engaging.

Start Smart

Use your first several posts to establish the type of information that interests you and you are likely to share over time. Prospective followers will look at your previous messages to learn if they want to follow you in the future.

Post Regularly

Build a loyal community of followers who look forward to learning with you. Post once a day, several times each day, or whatever your schedule (and attention span) supports. Because people use Twitter around the world, someone is always looking at it.

Keep Posts Short

With space for only 140 characters, don't waste words. Enlist the help of a thesaurus and learn some texting abbreviations. When you include links to a website, use a URL shortener like http://bit.ly. When you do write, mix up the post types to include retweets (RT), @replies, original thoughts, and links to other people's content.

Follow Carefully

Identify a few people who share your interests and follow them. Look at their homepages to see who they engage with and whom they follow. Find other people by searching topics you care about. On Twitter, seek out companies, competitors, and leaders in your industry to see how they use these tools. In your organization, look for people in other departments, different locations, or outside your usual sphere.

Go Mobile

Seek Twitter applications specifically designed for mobile devices so you can tweet on the go. What you lose in surface area, you gain in convenience.

Engage

When you see a post that catches your interest or asks a question, respond. Contribute. Add to the conversation. Once you have followers, check the @replies in the margin of your homepage to see who is connecting with you.

List

On Twitter and internal systems with a similar feature, create a list with the account names of people who are interested in a specific topic. This allows you to quickly focus on just their posts. Look at the lists of those you follow to see who else you might want to follow or to keep track of the posts of whom they follow.

Get Savvy

After you experiment with Twitter for a while, you may find it more convenient to use a third-party application that works with Twitter to manage your followers and your stream of bursts. Search the Internet for various tools to help you get the most from your Twitter experience. oneforty (http://oneforty.com) is an online directory and store for tools specifically created for use with Twitter. Most are free and easy to download.

Be Yourself

Microsharing works best when you represent yourself in an authentic way. One hundred and forty characters offer no extra space to spin messages or hype products (although plenty of people try). Share with people what you are thinking, what you need, and how together you can create sparks.

Growing Collective Intelligence

Collaborative tools are the breathing organisms that reflect the living nature of organizations today.

—Don Burke
Intellipedia Doyen, CIA

◆ ◆ ◆

On July 7, 2005, three bombs exploded within 50 seconds of one another on three London subways. A fourth went off an hour later in a double-decker bus on a busy downtown square. Together the bombs killed 56 people, including the four bombers, injuring nearly 700 people within the span of one morning rush hour, putting security agencies worldwide on high alert. Sean Dennehy watched the "7/7" events unfold from the headquarters of the U.S. Central Intelligence Agency outside Washington, D.C.[1]

Dennehy had recently received approval to pursue a small, classified wiki project and, along with senior CIA analyst Calvin Andrus, offered to be the pilot customer for an intelligence-community-wide wiki being readied for deployment. *Wiki* (Hawaiian for *quick*) allows a group to make changes to a shared web page.

Dennehy couldn't help but compare how rapidly Wikipedia, the largest wiki in the world, had synthesized information on the bombing with the traditional intelligence process of analysts individually reaching out to contacts, writing reports, and posting them in individual agency systems. Overlap was everywhere, each person focusing on the needs of the agency he or she serves while also defining the larger environment and scope of the event.

The year before, Andrus wrote a report called "The Wiki and the Blog: Toward a Complex Adaptive Intelligence Community," detailing the need for the intelligence community to adapt to the increased pace of the world.[2] With these new tools, intelligence community analysts could extend existing processes of idea generation and dialogue to the web with only a few mouse clicks. He laid out the wide-ranging intelligence benefit from collaborative tools with user-generated content.

What the United States needed after September 11, Andrus argued, was something that could handle rapidly changing, complicated threats. Intelligence organizations needed to become adaptive, driven to judgments by bottom-up collaboration, similar to financial markets or ant colonies—or Wikipedia.

For decades, the U.S. intelligence system had been structured to answer static or slowly developing, Cold War–era questions, such as the status of Soviet missile deployments or the construction of Soviet nuclear submarines. What the United States needed after September 11, Andrus argued, was something that could handle rapidly changing, complicated threats. Intelligence organizations needed to become adaptive, driven to judgments by bottom-up collaboration, similar to financial markets or ant colonies—or Wikipedia.

The Wikipedia model didn't seem like a perfect match, but it looked like an interesting way for intelligence analysts to capture, share, and cross-reference reports of situations in the world. In intelligence organizations, as in politics or the news business, what's new and captivating gains more attention than core information it's believed everyone should already know. Some pages of the wiki would contain active analysis. Others would contain reports of past activities that might provide useful context for current situations.

Dennehy believed a wiki model could capture and integrate stories and define issues in a way that also showed contributors and readers what had been written, added, and edited previously and that wasn't academic in its approach. It could also give people in the future contextualized insights and a way to reference other people's work without repeating the same peripheral details.

Around that same time, intelligence analyst Don Burke was looking at the changing nature of analysis and how the CIA could do a better job capturing its knowledge. As part of that activity, he began learning about wikis and started contributing to an internal CIA wiki. When Burke learned about Dennehy's work, he began editing and playing with the new, still in-pilot intelligence community wiki, now named Intellipedia.[3]

Soon Burke and Dennehy began bumping into one another within the wiki, both writing about the power of collaboration and laying philosophical and procedural roadmaps to how the tool could best be used by the intelligence community. Online they discussed meeting in person and were surprised to learn they worked in the same building. By the time they met face to face, though, they'd already solidified their partnership. When Burke's project ended and Intellipedia was officially unveiled to the intelligence community, he was reassigned from his management position to partner with Dennehy on pursuing Intellipedia full time.

Five years after the July 7 bombings in London, intelligence reports about the events still exist. Some are retrievable, but few offer people the ability to analyze similar stories and glean patterns and insights that might help prevent further incidents. Those who wrote the 7/7 reports moved on to the next target, the next project. Their earlier intelligence was considered "finished," although it did little to establish historical knowledge or provide cohesion with the larger organization, practices that are basic for transformative change. Reports often did not name their authors, due to counterintelligence concerns, so other analysts had no idea whom to contact for additional background.

In the past, each of the hundreds of reports about any crisis lived on its own. Even when coordination occurred, a report written to meet the specific needs of a customer might contain fundamentally the same information as other reports but not reach the same conclusions. This meant that each reader had to find and synthesize hundreds of documents and determine what was different or the same to get the intelligence community's perspective on an issue. There was simply too much information to sort through and synthesize in a useful way.

Dennehy, Burke, and about 30 others used the widely read Andrus paper, the first National Intelligence Strategy, recommendations from the 9/11 and Iraq Weapons of Mass Destruction (WMD) Commissions, and other documents to introduce Intellipedia across the intelligence community. Although the Andrus paper spelled out the many reasons why it would be an asset for national security, cultural resistance and pushback were stiff. Initially, analysts who were asked to participate said they were too busy or just preferred the old proprietary databases managed by individual agencies.

Others didn't see this collaborative and social approach fitting their mission-driven organizations because it wouldn't be easy to measure the impact of crowd-sourced entries. An individual focus is a powerful way to keep people on track, but detrimental because it's so tactical and lacks vision.

> When Sean Dennehy and Don Burke were tasked with increasing knowledge sharing across the intelligence community in 2005, it was like being asked to promote vegetarianism in Texas. Against the odds, these analysts in the Central Intelligence Agency succeeded in promoting a tool that breaks with the prevailing culture, increases the flow of information, and ultimately contributes to making the United States safer.

One big hurdle was convincing security-minded people that the system would be safe from outsiders. To allay concerns, Intellipedia was built into the existing secure and classified network known as *Intelink*, which connects the intelligence agencies in the United States, the U.S. military, the Department of State, and other agencies with access to intelligence.

The vision was to break down barriers to information sharing and capturing knowledge, demonstrating that intelligence knows no geographic boundaries.

Years later, now a sanctioned initiative with tens of thousands of registered users and upward of 10,000 page edits a day, Intellipedia gets people what they need and when they need it. In 2009, traffic on Intellipedia became so heavy that the Office of the Director of National Intelligence had to find extra money to upgrade its servers.

The site's real-time, user-generated content has proven pivotal in the unfolding of several major events. For example, in February 2007 when Iraqi insurgents conducted several attacks incorporating chlorine into an improvised explosive device, someone created a wiki page asking what intelligence officers and others in the field should do to collect evidence of chlorine use. Twenty-three people at locations around the world chimed in to create a serviceable set of instructions in two days. No time was wasted on meetings.

Another example of a visible change in learning and practice came as a result of 10 Islamic militants overrunning two hotels in Mumbai, India, on November 26, 2008. Analysts stationed around the world immediately converged on a newly created Intellipedia page about the attacks, which they updated continuously as new information came to light. Over the course of the three-day standoff, the page logged more than 7,000 views and was integral to understanding and analyzing the attack.

Intellipedia doesn't aim to produce "finished" analysis—a term used widely in the intelligence community to imply completed reports for decision makers. Those are still written the old-fashioned way and circulated for peer review and consensus. Instead, Intellipedia encompasses a constantly changing world that can never be complete but can provide lessons at any time.

During the Beijing Olympics, a personal matter prevented an analyst from writing the official reports on the events, but the information he had contributed to Intellipedia over the previous years provided invaluable analysis to those who did write the reports. When the topic of Beijing surged, others in the intelligence community had a place to start and a context that kept them from coming in cold. Thousands of examples such as these, showing that people who are connected are more powerful than any number working alone, are needed until this way of working becomes part of the intelligence-gathering fabric.

Intellipedia doesn't aim to produce "finished" analysis—a term used widely in the intelligence community to imply completed reports for decision makers. Those are still written the old-fashioned way and circulated for peer review and consensus. Instead, Intellipedia encompasses a constantly changing world that can never be complete but can provide lessons at any time. The online intelligence encyclopedia can also provide more accurate data than in the past because a wide range of experts, who help keep the material current and accurate, can scrutinize and amend what's written.

The CIA is only one of the U.S. intelligence, diplomatic, and military organizations that use Intellipedia on top secret, secret, and unclassified networks. Burke and Dennehy have been two of the most visible proponents of this new model, but Intellipedia's success derives from a core group of advocates who have quietly worked within their organizations to demonstrate and articulate how Intellipedia can be used to improve the mission of the intelligence community.

Managed by the Office of the Director of National Intelligence (DNI), Intellipedia captures current conditions by giving broad access and updating rights to 16 agencies of the U.S. intelligence community. In 2008, Intellipedia access rights were given to state and local law enforcement officials so they could benefit from relevant, up-to-date intelligence.

Deploying and keeping Intellipedia active is no easy task, though, when it's outside people's daily routines. At times, Dennehy who is now the Intellipedia and Enterprise 2.0 evangelist, knows some analysts may have informative conversations on Intellipedia and then have to document the exchange on an agency's official system, too.

Intelligence analysis should be a process of working on problems and trying to get sharper at them. Intellipedia is ideal for that. Greg Treverton, director of the Rand Corporation's Center for Global Risk and Security, says, "If you slice it at any given time, you are saying, 'Here is the best state of understanding at the moment.'"[4]

Dennehy points out that, "It's important to look at how we get to the finished intelligence. Intellipedia does this by making the process more social and creating a dialogue that's transparent."

"In addition to analysis, we need people who can create an ecosystem of knowledge that is not specifically about answering tomorrow's questions, but creating a world of information that is connected," adds Burke. "It feels alive."

Intellipedia is largely managed by volunteers and watched over by "shepherds" who answer questions and keep track of individual pages in their areas of expertise. Like Wikipedia, the authorship of articles is clear: There are no cryptic user names to hide behind. People can find and learn where ideas come from fast.

Intellipedia has become a shining light of possibility for a better way to work thanks to the countless contributions from individuals who post blogs, edit Intellipedia, tag pages, and persuade others to try these tools. It represents the efforts of thousands of intelligence and national security professionals, who often had to swim upstream against a culture of status quo. It allows federal agents to share information, intelligence, evidence, tips, and background information across agency boundaries and serves as a hub where people can quickly glean details that matter to their work.

Intellipedia is largely managed by volunteers and watched over by "shepherds" who answer questions and keep track of individual pages in their areas of expertise. Like Wikipedia, the authorship of articles is clear: There are no cryptic user names to hide behind. People can find and learn where ideas come from fast.

Intellipedia begins to peel away the old need-to-know mentality and enables a need-to-share culture. It builds a case that collaboration has an impact on how situations unfold.

Increase Collective IQ

Watch a group of four-year-olds build a skyscraper made of cardboard, and you might think anything is possible. One offers up her vision, another gets the boxes, and a third clears the space in anticipation of something big. No one taught them their roles or pointed out the opportunity. They each saw something greater than they could do alone (or at least in the time before playgroup ends), and they joined in, *collectively*.

Collaboration is something we've known how to do our entire lives. Working together to produce something more significant than one person can do alone is timeless.

Modern collaboration tools, when used by several people simultaneously, enable a shift in individual thinking about the energy and intelligence we can produce together. Add to that the complex nature and urgency of problems facing organizations today, which are increasing faster than individual capabilities to understand and cope with them, and it's clear why we should take advantage of collaboration tools to work collectively.

> *To support keeping information current, create systems that support updates and contributions from many people who are affected or who have additional perspectives—where the group can capture, organize, share, and use its emerging and dynamic knowledge.*

"If you ask someone what data they want to share with whom, in a general fashion, people give up, overwhelmed," says Adina Levin, collaborative software visionary and cofounder of Socialtext. "But when tools enable people to share information about themselves, their organizations, and the urgent issues they face right now in the context of who they are meeting with and what they are working on, people make pretty good decisions and create real digital social networks."[5]

This chapter introduces both the opportunities and challenges for people working together to develop outcomes reflective of right now and supporting the large world around them. Working together isn't something new; capturing perception, thinking, and the ideas needed to understand the full context of a problem and produce something that remains up to date is revolutionary.

Published works represent points frozen in time. When an analyst at the CIA develops "finished intelligence" or an analyst firm writes about the state of wikis in a traditional report, the information is instantly dated. It might be extremely valuable, but the second it's printed it is no longer fresh.

To support keeping information current, create systems that support updates and contributions from many people who are affected or who have additional perspectives—where the group can capture, organize, share, and use its emerging and dynamic knowledge. This leads to both living content and the means to come together to quickly and intelligently anticipate or respond to a situation, leveraging collective perception.

Living content tools (those in the general wiki category or specific tools such as Google Docs or DimDim) can be thought of as malleable publishing platforms. They are less structured technologies than those used to create online communities, or to support media- and microsharing. They can fulfill many different objectives for collaborating, teaching, recording, and learning.

Their success should be measured not by how many people use them but by a finer outcome: developing something broader, deeper, or more innovative than individuals could create on their own. Value grows from the ability to embody content that seems alive, morphing over time to represent the current state of what's known and the status of a network's capability to identify and act on what's relevant.

Doug Engelbart, the father of personal computing and an advocate for over a half century for the creation of collaborative tools to augment collective work, believes the answers are right in front of us—if only we could reach them.[6] What if groups of people could access their collective knowledge quickly when facing a decision, sorting through all other noise, and keying in on the most relevant information? It would vastly improve our ability to deal with complex, urgent problems—to get the best possible understanding of a situation, including the best possible solutions.

The success of any size organization or team is based on its collective IQ, a measure of how well people work *collectively* on important problems and challenges. It becomes a measure of how effective we are at tackling complex, urgent problems and opportunities and how effectively a group can concurrently develop, integrate, and apply its knowledge toward its mission.

Share for Our Time

The power of collaborative content tools is in their ability to offer a single destination where people bring their ideas together, vet them with their peers, and publish them in a way that they can be revised and revisited, representing multiple viewpoints.

For the social media tools that can be used for learning and working together, codifying the multifaceted nature of information, Burke and Dennehy have identified three qualities that stand out as markers of success: vibrancy, socialness, and relevance.

Tools in Use

Jesse Wilson, who works at the U.S. Central Command's Afghanistan Pakistan Intelligence Center of Excellence, describes his work with living tools this way:

I use these tools in several ways, but I'll give three examples. First, I track issues I'm responsible for every day. Everyone in my group has a choice: to either save that information in folders only accessible to a department, or to put that knowledge into department-neutral, issue-based pages. I've chosen the latter. And when others do this, you not only pool the community's collective knowledge, but you also begin to build a social network of other people working on the same issues.

I'll give you an example. A certain issue popped up. Rather than releasing an updated report every week, we integrated our knowledge into a wiki page, which was up in a matter of seconds, and invited as many people as possible to contribute. Over the course of several months, that page was edited 500 times and viewed more than 12,000 times by people all across the community. We had 13 offices contributing to the page. It was amazing.

We also use it to track our team's weekly activities and productivity. Friday used to be the day when everyone scrambled to compile a list of what they did over the course of the week, usually by sending a thread of emails back and forth and eventually compiling a list to send to our boss to send to his boss. Now, instead, our team adds things to a page throughout the week, and on Friday we simply send the link to our boss.

Finally, the other way I use the wiki is to upload large files that I don't want to email out to hundreds of people and fill up their inboxes. Instead, I upload the file and email the link. This is a much more efficient way of sharing knowledge.

Source: J. Wilson, interview with authors, 2009.

Vibrancy

Living content tools, similar to their social counterparts such as online communities, media-sharing sites, and even microsharing spaces, are measured by their vibrancy and their ability to energize the people who use them. They showcase people's needs, interests, passions, and emotions.

Vibrancy characterizes the inviting, energizing place where people want to be. The space is jumping, alive with energy. People come back because they find value.

Envision a party. When you walk in, it takes only a few seconds to judge if you want to be there and if it has taken off. People are exceptionally good at assessing this. It's primordial. We have millions of years of evolution in our DNA telling us to be wary of a dead place where we stand out, where we wonder, "Is it precarious for me to be here?"

When a collaborative space is hopping with activity, form follows content, not the other way around. Planning revolves around how to get more "eyes on content" to improve accuracy, add perspective and subtleties, and show it has captured what's new.

This poses a chicken-and-egg problem, though. Someone has to create the vibrancy, open the space, and welcome the guests. Someone has to get the ball rolling. Intellipedia became successful because initially a core group of people was willing to contribute before there was any reason to do so, before the other participants arrived.

NASA's Spacebook, an online community for collaboration and sharing resources, became successful because its developer, Emma Antunes, the Goddard Space Flight Center web manager, specifically sought user-generated content. Spacebook's earliest features were a general discussion group, a place for new employees to meet, and an equipment exchange forum, similar to Craigslist. They were created first because people could immediately see a personal benefit and an organizational success from every addition.[7]

At NASA, the challenge of encouraging adoption and active participation—vibrancy—was sky high because the site encouraged communication and collaboration outside the bureaucratic channels people knew.

Socialness

If, as Woody Allen said, 80 percent of success is showing up, at least 10 percent of the remaining 20 requires engaging with those around you who can contribute to your success.

If people don't talk and support each other and build off one another, social tools don't provide much benefit. Interaction among people amplifies individual contributions. Articles on similar subjects can change from noise to sound when they're synthesized and cross-linked.

The chipmaker Intel has a rich collaborative wiki environment, which is called—you guessed it—Intelpedia. Started in 2005, it is the epitome of socialness. With more than 44,000 total pages, topics range from the Intel Acronym Dictionary to tips on giving presentations and include more than 13,000 files uploaded from business groups.

The success of the wiki led to increased visibility for social computing and to Intel's launch of Planet Blue, an online professional networking and community tool. Employees now have personal homepages with contact information and biographical data, lively discussions, and places for groups to congregate as they work together. An authoritative *listen only to the expert* culture has transformed into one that hears experts alongside novices, reaching around the world and surfacing creative solutions to the newest challenges.

With more than 125 million page views, more than 325,000 page edits, more than seven average edits per page, and more than 380 views per edit, it seems that socialness is leading the way on Intelpedia.

One of the most active groups in the space is Intel's Learning community of practice, pulling together people from business groups across the globe that care about the topic of learning. With more than 50 training groups and even more people working in unidentified training roles, connecting everyone in the learning community has been impossible. Now, however, 320 of the more than 1,000 employees in the learning community have joined together in a global conversation. When someone asks a question, it's seconds, not minutes or hours, until someone responds.

A year after a very popular career development workshop, a collaborative community was created for those who continued to be interested in the topic. Employees share thoughts, questions, and even career opportunities as they take what they learned about themselves in the workshop and apply that knowledge to their daily work.

The PERL Programming Community is only one of several dozen collaborative spaces for programmers and engineers to share tips across all of Intel's geographies, cutting down the time it takes them to be competent in their roles and to find solutions. Along the way, they document leading-edge practices, explore new ideas, and update one another on how their work is changing.

Another collaborative community is Intel Learning and Development, a group of about 200 people across the globe. Since creating the community, members have stopped all mass emails except those that point to discussions happening in other parts of Planet Blue. Their periodic "all hands" meetings now also have an online component.

> *Allison Anderson, program manager for learning innovation at Intel, points out that with these collaborative spaces and vibrant conversations, organizations can go far beyond benchmarking, a practice that captures what came before.*

Allison Anderson, program manager for learning innovation at Intel, points out that with these collaborative spaces and vibrant conversations, organizations can go far beyond benchmarking, a practice that captures what came before.[8]

Relevance

What good are vibrant social exchanges if they aren't pertinent to the people and mission of your organization?

Four years of double-digit growth has made training and retaining talent a priority for T. Rowe Price Group, the Baltimore-based investment management firm. It has also made Michael McDermott, vice president of learning and organization development, a very busy guy. Rather than create more traditional courses, he worked with the IT group to launch Discovery, a company-wide, wiki-based, collaborative knowledge management tool that incorporates online forums, RSS feeds, bookmarking, tagging, and search.

With Discovery, associates can ask difficult research questions and capture answers, creating new and emerging categories of relevant information. The program has increased the ability to publish and update information quickly. The robust search capabilities reduce the turnaround time for answers to research questions and leverage for future use all the information being submitted.

Discovery also serves as the infrastructure for one of the few new courses they've built, Building Change Capability, where associates can access a dedicated wiki site, blogs, and other social media tools to supplement the course materials; have ongoing conversations; and add to the course content so it gets better and more applicable over time.[9]

Taken together, a site's degree of vibrancy, socialness, and relevance offer a distinctive way to evaluate the success of a collaborative environment. More powerfully though, these criteria can serve as objective measurements of the quality and reputation of a person's or group's contributions. Are people contributing? How, when, where, and how often? Are they interacting in a positive way? Sentiment analysis could even be applied. Does editing have a positive tone? Are people discussing, cross-linking, and debating in a healthy way?

Such measures allow organizations to evaluate employees not by their direct output (number of reports, accounts won, or hours on the job) but by how well they facilitate and enable a virtual collaborative community and contribute to something larger than themselves.

Break with the Past

Emerging technology and the need for speed drive the creation of living content sites. Many of the most active and successful environments, including Intellipedia and Intelpedia, have embraced the new technology and the culture that comes with it by overcoming organizational hurdles. Here are three principles developed in 2006 by Dennehy and Burke that helped chart Intellipedia's growth and may benefit you too.

Now or Then?

These were items in the Office of Strategic Services' (the precursor to the CIA) *Simple Sabotage Field Manual*, published in 1944. Now declassified, it reads almost like a manual of how some organizations operate today and hints at why living content meets resistance.

Do the statements below reflect characteristics of your organization?

- ◆ Insist on doing everything through channels. Never permit shortcuts that would expedite decisions.
- ◆ When possible, refer all matters to committees for "further study and consideration."
- ◆ Haggle over precise wording of communications.
- ◆ Advocate caution and reason so as to avoid embarrassment.
- ◆ Question whether a decision lies within the jurisdiction of the group or whether it might conflict with the policy of some higher echelon.

Source: U.S. Office of Strategic Services, *Simple Sabotage Field Manual* (Washington, DC: OSS, 1944), retrieved June 20, 2010 at http://www.gutenberg.org/etext/26184.

Think Topically, Not Organizationally

Is your organization too siloed? In a rigid hierarchy, it can be difficult to meet the fast-changing needs of the marketplace because it takes precious time to move up and down the chain of command (if it's even possible) to develop relevant relationships or access vital information.

Joe Sullivan, an extreme problem solver in the corporate scientific community, finds that organizations lull themselves into a false sense of safety with their hierarchies rather than recognize the danger of discouraging information flow, keeping data out of the minds of people who need it.[10] In a way similar to the inevitable errors in childhood games of telephone, information can become diluted and ambiguous, filtered and repackaged, or at worst incorrect when it only flows one way.

The Intellipedians constantly have to guard against new contributors who are inclined to tag their entries in Intellipedia based on the agency of origin so their organization can "get credit." For example, a page on former Cuban president Fidel Castro might be tagged in the subject header as coming from the Federal Bureau of Investigation, although the FBI is not the subject of the article; that tag doesn't help others find the document when seeking information on Castro.

A single source of aggregated information on a topic serves the larger community better because it helps eliminate territoriality of authorship. Debate can focus on the topic instead of who said what in which organization. When working topically, each organization can add what it knows to a common page—and then, if necessary, create subpages or articles unique to their group.

With many people noticing what has changed, what ought to be challenged, or what pertains to colleagues elsewhere, information can be amended and repurposed for better accuracy, currency, and wider value.

When the shared space includes information that can be easily linked, searched, and tagged, anyone new to the organization or to a task can get up to speed quickly on a topic or teach a class about it, can find previous discussions and debates, and see its status as it lives today.

Work with the Broadest Possible Audience

Is your organization too myopic? When working in a collaborative system, people are encouraged to work with the broadest audience possible, which runs counter to many organizations' prevailing culture of specialization amid need to know.

Without collaborative alternatives, people duplicate work because information is lost in shared drives and old emails. It can be eye opening to participate in a virtual community and realize we're not the only ones doing particular work or who have the information and insights others need.

The broadest possible audience is the widest network to which an individual has access. Where sensitive issues are concerned, build hubs of information for the far-reaching audience and then move to more restricted space for sensitive information.

In Intellipedia, users can create links among environments, a process called "creating breadcrumbs," leading from where you came to where you're going. The network can then control access. If a person has access, they will be able to follow the link. If they don't, they at least know that more information exists, and they can begin following the breadcrumbs.

Replace Existing Processes

Is your organization too habit-focused? Social tools present an opportunity to replace old, time-consuming processes with faster ones.

Let's say you and your co-workers need to compile and synthesize a lot of information every day. Instead of working individually to gather data from shared drives, folders, and work documents, you can do this work in a wiki. Instead of using email to debate an idea, you can use blogs. Instead of using your browser's "favorites" list, you can use social tagging. Instead of storing files in a shared folder behind a firewall that is not indexed by search engines, you can use a shared document repository.

You might believe you are too busy to learn a new tool or to deposit information in more than one place, but replacing your current processes with new, more efficient ones is not adding more duties.

IBM uses a wiki-based tool specifically for capturing knowledge from retiring workers. Dubbed "Pass It Along," the wiki allows employees to post their knowledge and create tutorials for people coming up behind them.

Living content tools such as Pass It Along and Intelpedia provide a way to help new employees understand how the company operates and familiarize themselves with its various systems. It does this in the context of the people who have walked those systems for years, noticing the subtleties and the obvious roads mapped in handbooks and training classes.

Teresita Abay-Krueger, a marketing executive with IBM's software developer outreach program, says, "From the point of view of an enterprise decision maker, you need to onboard employees quickly and uniformly. Pass It Along is an effective way to give new employees a tool for understanding how the company operates and the legacy systems it has."[11]

Respond to Critics

Do these ideas and practices sound appealing but you know others will have objections you will need to address? Here are the common questions we receive when introducing the living content approach and how we address them.

Finished Content Is More Valuable than Works in Progress

There is a spectrum of knowledge that goes from the most nascent early stages of information up to polished presentable deliverable content—in the form of a report, presentation, web page, and more. If your organization relies on the sale or distribution of products that capture a situation on a certain date, consider the content created in a living tool such as a wiki as complementary rather than competing. Collaborative spaces are where people in your organization can synthesize issues, ideas, arguments, and actions into coherent, meaningful messages and learn from one another as they produce a product for a customer at a particular moment. These spaces become a venue for enhancing the thoroughness and comprehensiveness of the product.

At EMC, work-in-progress content is more valuable than finished content because it shows how the organization arrived at where it is, which is often a key element that employees, customers, partners, prospects, and even the media are keenly interested in. Works in progress also show EMC stakeholders that there is room for improvement and room for commentary, and, in fact, both are welcomed. This exposure makes the organization more vulnerable and yet seem more human when not everything that comes out is polished and professional. It provides insight into the organization that might not have otherwise been gleaned and, in turn, offers stakeholders more reason to trust the organization because it has shown how it works.

It's Risky to Let Anyone Post Anything

In a wiki, all posts are attributed to the person who makes them. They are more discoverable than emails or a bulletin board where rumors or innuendo can circulate forever without attribution. This transparency makes it a lot easier to spot people who are posting things they shouldn't and address their comments or inappropriate behavior quickly.

Perhaps more important, contributors can actually build a reputation on the site. This becomes an incentive for some to adopt the tools, actively participate, and publish high-quality content, knowing they may gain the attention of leaders and others working in complementary roles throughout the organization.

Our Information Is Unique; There Is No Way to Share That

The uniqueness of information is precisely why it should be shared in flexible systems. Unique information doesn't fit neatly into document management systems that enforce rigid workflows and archiving rules. Living content tools can have templates that impose some consistency, but beyond that, they can be freeform and open to presentation specific to the characteristics of the content or conversation itself.

We Have a Wiki But Only a Few People Contribute Articles

If people believe that creating Microsoft Word documents and sending them around in email works better than using a wiki, consider converting a few documents to the wiki and sending around a link where people can find and edit them online. Next time, people may try posting documents to the wiki first.

Stuart Mader, author of *Wikipatterns*, suggests a wiki "barnraising"— a planned event in which a community meets at a designated time to build content on the wiki together. A barnraising gives people a chance to learn how to use the wiki while interacting with others as they work, strengthening community bonds and creating a support network that keeps people using the wiki.[12]

Eugene Eric Kim, founder of Blue Oxen Associates, a think tank focused on improving collaboration, points out that "People seem to get very caught up with getting *everyone* engaged. If you install a wiki in your organization of 100 people and only five are actively using it, some might see that as a failure. I have never seen a great social tool go from zero to everybody overnight. With large groups, you will always see a power law of participation, where only a small percentage of people are actively contributing. And there will be plenty to learn from that participation."[13]

Recommendations

Begin to publish online in an open, organic way. When people in your organization can begin collaborating with the assistance of online tools and make their work visible, current, and available to everyone, doors will open to wider participation and more vibrant, social, and relevant results. Here are some first steps.

Be Bold

Be bold in updating whatever you read in your wiki or other shared tools. Momentum builds faster when people fix problems, correct grammar, add facts, make sure the language is precise, and so on. How many times have you read something on a website and thought, "Well, that's wrong. Why doesn't somebody fix that?" Collaborative systems not only allow you to add, revise, and edit an article—they encourage you to do it. It does require some amount of politeness, but it works. You'll see. And of course, others will edit what you write. Don't take it personally. They, like all of us, just want to make the results as good as they can possibly be.

Don't Be Reckless

Being bold in updating pages does not mean that you should make large changes or deletions to long articles on complex, controversial subjects with long histories, without careful thought. The text may be the result of long and arduous negotiations among people of diverse backgrounds and points of view. Before you edit an article, first read it all, read the comments, and view the page history to get a sense of how the article came into being and what its current status is. It's also worth reading some related articles to see if what you thought was a problem or an omission has already been addressed.

Begin Where You Are

Because shared spaces need people to start conversations, consider starting with topics that you care deeply about, things you want others' perspectives on and that would help in your work. These are the topics you will be the most motivated to invest time in.

Have a Sense of Play

Experiment with new ideas; learn by trying and doing rather than expecting the first piece of content you contribute to be perfect. A sense of play adds a personal, lighthearted tone to a space, even those used primarily for work-related collaboration. It just sets a tone and helps maintain an environment that feels authentic, personal, and human.

Gain Grassroots and Top-Down Sponsorship

Begin at whatever level works for your organization's culture. Some organizations respond best when people on the front line participate first. Others only get involved when they see senior leaders contributing. If you have early conversations with people from both groups, as well as those in the middle, you're more likely to garner the attention and participation of those who are curious but a little timid about jumping in.

Use the Crowd

A group can help keep its members on track through constant reinforcement of good practices, building and communicating guidelines, reverting or removing inappropriate material, and having continual social dialogue about the right balance. On rare occasions, organizations need to take action, but those are few and far between and usually, in the end, reflect more positively than negatively because they demonstrate the power of peers managing one another.

Ask Hard Questions

Asking a dull question takes as much time as asking a meaningful one, so ask those that get at information you and your organization need. "So, how far along are you with this idea?" Or, "Has anyone else succeeded in doing this?" Those who make the most effective members of a collaborative team are those who get to the heart of issues and facilitate effectively and honestly.

Collectively Apply Metadata Through Tagging

Tagging allows people to apply their own metadata to content and documents. Tagging also allows people to leverage tags others have already applied to a particular piece of content. The result is a collection of terms, a user-generated taxonomy or "folksonomy." In this way, people interested in certain topics, subtopics, and themes can come together to get their work done.

Don't Rely on Tools Alone

You can't make people collaborate just by making living content tools available. New practice and tools often come amid resistance. When copy machines, fax machines, email, and instant messaging were introduced, initially there was skepticism. But over time these tools were adopted because people saw their value and eventually their necessity.

Although individuals ultimately decide whether or not to use these tools, it's critical for organizations to adopt them because no one these days can gather the information he or she needs fast enough to respond to the quickening pace of work without them. Problems are becoming too complex for one person to solve; issues have too many tentacles to be understood fully by a single person. By augmenting the natural reaction to share interesting information, improve the work of others, and help organizations succeed, we create systems as alive as they are useful.

Chapter 6

Immersive Environments Refine Learning

"Virtual environments can provide more dimensions than physical environments and more social, nuanced ways for people to learn from one another as they face complex challenges."

—Kevyn Renner
Senior Technology Consultant, Chevron

♦ ♦ ♦

At a Chevron refinery, executives from around the world meet to talk about the future leadership of the organization. They discuss how the next generation can learn from the current leaders and how this will shape the workforce of the future. People from the organization development team sit along the periphery of the room, listening in and occasionally offering insights. Chevron is deeply committed to creating an innovative workplace, and this meeting is a vital step.

Then the unexpected happens. At the refinery where they sit, a major processing unit where gasoline is made has an unscheduled shutdown. The executives need to move from dialogue to action, making rapid decisions to determine what effect this shutdown will have on the facility, their people on staff at the refinery, the oil in the pipeline, and the environment. The facilitators stand by, recording as much as they can, because this could inform all aspects of their scenario planning.

Every minute counts. Every decision has a potentially global impact. Making the best decisions possible is job number one. There is no time to do anything but work together to respond. The executive team does so again and again, demonstrating the experience and decision-making ability that led them to their positions at Chevron.

They do so from their desks, in some instances thousands of miles from one another, though it feels like they are side by side. The oil refinery is in a virtual immersive environment created by Chevron to study, among other things, how company leaders make critical decisions and pass them on.

> *Kevyn Renner, senior technology consultant at Chevron, drives the company's efforts to apply new information technology in industry-changing ways. In Chevron's virtual environment developed by Renner and his team, participants can work in safety while facing authentic and potentially dangerous situations.*

At refineries, they may not be able to move pipes or vessels quickly, but they can move information fast. For example, a refinery can be accurately depicted in three dimensions (3D), serving as a proving ground for cutting-edge techniques and experiential learning.

Kevyn Renner, senior technology consultant at Chevron, drives the company's efforts to apply new information technology in industry-changing ways. In Chevron's virtual environment developed by Renner and his team, participants can work in safety while facing authentic and potentially dangerous situations. Their actions can also be captured, analyzed, and learned from by others. In the refinery shutdown instance, up-and-coming leaders can go through the shutdown scenario to learn on their feet and can then talk with the executive team about how to refine their practices. In this case, the upcoming leaders can make tactical decisions that the senior team can learn from. These social interactions can enhance Chevron's operational performance.[1]

Real-time sensor information fed into the model creates, in effect, a constantly updated 3D learning environment. With this intelligent model, experts from around the world, using avatars, can interact as if they were working in the same room.

Renner explains the value of the environment by way of analogy, showing a graph of sudden improvements in high jumping over the past 100 years, due to radical changes in technique from the scissors, to the western roll, to the straddle, and culminating in the famous "Fosbury Flop." This demonstrates the way innovation and new ideas mature. Often a spark of innovation leads to gradual evolution until the next spark. Sometimes the establishment will push back, but as the workplace fills with people who have always known immersive environments, the establishment will change.

New technology can enable dramatic improvements in outcome. That's especially true with immersive environments because they can provide far more dimensions than real environments. Every industry can find benefits in digital models, especially high-dollar manufacturing, infrastructure, and energy industries where working together in a realistic environment can be dangerous or impractical. It's as if a new planet is being constructed, and people can learn there immediately.

Renner talks about the virtual environment his team is piloting using the terminology of the oil refinery—not that of social media or language created for the 3D Internet. He describes it as a living environment, a lab where people work and learn together. He uses words that convey what people at work can do with the technology. For Chevron and many other organizations using similar techniques, these are collaboration spaces, operations centers, and building blocks rather than virtual worlds and objects or files in a 3D environment.

Practicing in real time in a realistic setting is vital for people development and learning in every company. The oil industry has at least one more reason to value such practice. The industry as a whole suffered a downturn in the 1980s and early 1990s and therefore didn't hire many people for a decade. This resulted in a talent and knowledge gap. As experienced team members retire, there is a shortage of people with long-term institutional knowledge to replace them.

The next generation of workers is coming into the workforce with networking and multiprocessing skills and a global mindedness their elders never would have imagined. Constant experience in the networked world has had a profound impact on their approach to problem solving and collaboration.

Renner uses the analogy of the kaleidoscope to describe the many perspectives that people experience when working in virtual spaces. It fits with the organization's mandate to have the *right people in the right place with the right talent*, so they can get work done in a timely and reliable way. The largest private producer of renewable energy and the sixth-largest company in the world based on revenues, Chevron takes education very seriously, consistent with its "Human Energy" philosophy.

> *The next generation of workers is coming into the workforce with networking and multiprocessing skills and a global mindedness their elders never would have imagined. Constant experience in the networked world has had a profound impact on their approach to problem solving and collaboration.*

Chevron wants its focus and activities to attract, develop, recognize, and retain people who help the organization produce top competitive results as the internal and external environment changes. Climbing into a virtual world allows them to do that realistically, safely, and repeatedly. The virtual environment supports remote collaboration, real-time immersion, and expert knowledge capture. It is the application and approach to innovative technology that gives Chevron one of its competitive advantages.

"We have a very complex environment in the refining industry," says Renner. "The next-generation control room provides a collaborative work environment for making better decisions based on situational awareness, which affects safety, reliability, and overall performance. Cloud computing and virtual immersive environments help provide a contextual view of the operating plant. Oil and gas firms can derive actionable information from multiple data sources and thereby lay a foundation for a proactive and predictive operating philosophy."

Get Together Virtually

People increasingly need to work and learn together even when they can't physically be together. Sometimes asynchronous communication is enough. You write email, then you send it to someone who reads it and responds, or you post a tweet or something new to the online community. Other times, a real-time interaction works best. Trouble is, traditional tools such as audio conferencing, videoconferencing, and web conferencing usually provide a significantly poorer experience than face-to-face interaction because they lack some of the sensory dimensions people rely on to read situations.

Technologies are emerging to create the illusion that people are physically together in the same place at the same time. The best examples are telepresence and virtual immersive environments.

Virtual immersive environments are a category of emerging technologies that encompass virtual worlds, gaming, and simulations that have a social component and closely mirror working with someone in the same physical space.

"This is an umbrella term for whole categories of tools that overlap and blur in feature design and technical functionality," points out Koreen Olbrish, CEO of immersive consultancy Tandem Learning. "What makes them unique is that each represents a different type of experience. Virtual worlds mirror a universe around you, simulations offer goal-based activities, and games feature layers of competition. The lines are blurred when simulations are games, or virtual worlds contain games or simulations working together to create an immersive experience."[2]

Immersive refers to a sense of surrounding ourselves in something, a space in which we are present. We can immerse ourselves in a sport, a

---

What Is Included in Virtual Immersive Environments?

Virtual immersive environments encompass

- ♦ virtual worlds
- ♦ gaming
- ♦ simulations.

---

hobby, work, or an environment. The degree of immersion is important because the more we feel like we're in the environment, the more likely we are to feel engaged. What makes virtual immersive environments unique is that we emerge from them with real-life experiences we've actually participated in, not just imagined.

"Think IMAX movies, surround sound, and World of Warcraft applied to the web and business applications," says Erica Driver, industry analyst and cofounder of ThinkBalm. "What these all have in common is that they engage—even engross—the people using them."[3]

Virtual Worlds

Virtual worlds are online representations of reality you step through as you would the physical world. They can also stretch the usual bounds of the real world, providing an opportunity to glimpse what's going on behind a wall or across the globe.

Virtual worlds have become second homes for millions of people worldwide. And they aren't just for kids. Businesses use these environments for training and recruitment. Conferences and reunions are held "in world." Ideas are tested. Debates play out. People learn to work in a virtual space where they can innovate, connect, reorganize, and redeploy hundreds or thousands of people around specific activities, enabling them to self-organize based on interests, objectives, or skills.

These environments can be the stage for other social media tools, or they can be features within online communities or media-sharing sites, adding an immersive and engaging visual element to a two- or three-dimensional experience.

Like the Star Trek *holodeck*, virtual worlds are a clean canvas where designers can create a digital simulated experience in which people interact with their environment and with other people in the virtual space. The designer's challenge is to figure out what to create and where people can interact.

Virtual worlds are particularly useful when people need to engage in multisite meetings or multiparty conversations, especially when visual cues and nonverbal communication are particularly important. They prove quite useful for "virtual field trips" and offsite meetings and don't require ever leaving the building. They are also a natural choice when you need to show 3D data-like models of buildings or parts to go into manufactured products or molecular structures, or when people need training for work in hazardous environments.

John Seely Brown, visiting scholar at the University of Southern California and former chief scientist at Xerox, and Douglas Thomas, who teaches at USC's Annenberg School for Communication and edits *Games & Culture: A Journal of Interactive Media,* believe at base that these are learning environments. "This kind of learning is radically different from what we traditionally think of as learning: the accumulation of facts or acquisition of knowledge. They involve the experience of acting together to overcome obstacles, managing skills, talents, and relationships, and they create contexts in which social awareness, reflection, and joint coordinated action become an essential part of the experience, providing the basis for a networked imagination."[4]

Virtual worlds enable a physical sense of being together, working together, interacting in real time, seeing one another, and sharing space. In that sense, virtual worlds are similar to other new social learning approaches that provide a means—in this case a place—for transferring

---

Four Criteria of Virtual Worlds

Although there are different types of virtual worlds, Koreen Olbrish explains they have four criteria in common:

- **Shared space:** A virtual world must portray a sense of being in proximity to and provide the ability to roam around objects and avatars.
- **Persistence:** Even when people aren't logged in, the virtual world still exists. When a participant leaves, the virtual world continues to evolve, just as the real world does.
- **Immediacy:** Activities in a virtual world operate in real time. When we're in it, we're in it together, synchronously.
- **Interactivity:** Every virtual world gives visitors some degree of control over the environment—at least the ability to interact with other avatars and the world itself.

Source: K. Olbrish, Interview with authors, 2009.

knowledge among people in organizations, allowing them to understand a situation, and even constructing an idea or a structure together. The activities within these virtual places make coordination and interaction possible and necessary.

Games

Some virtual environments take the form of massive multiplayer online role-playing games (MMOG). Not just fun, these multiplayer online games help players develop and exercise skills closely matching the planning, learning, and technical skills increasingly needed in the workplace. Playing can require strategic thinking, interpretative analysis, problem solving, formulating plans, team building, cooperating, and adapting to rapid change.

> *Virtual worlds enable a physical sense of being together, working together, interacting in real time, seeing one another, and sharing space.*

Tony O'Driscoll, executive director of Fuqua's Center for IT and Media at Duke University and co-author of *Learning in 3D*, was part of a research team in 2008 that found that the skills necessary to lead in games closely resemble those necessary to lead in the real world, identifying and leveraging our organization's competitive advantage while making quick decisions based on large amounts of fast-moving information. For example, the U.S. Army offers a 3D virtual video game called *America's Army*, which lets participants crawl through obstacle courses, fire weapons, and engage in paratrooper actions—without leaving their chairs. What feels like a game is actually an army recruiting and training tool.[5]

Simulations

"A simulation is a digital model that represents situation or process. When a story gets wrapped around it and people are asked to do something in the simulation, you have a scenario," says Clark Quinn, author of *Engaging Learning: Designing e-Learning Simulation Games* and an upcoming book on mobile learning.[6] Simulations provide opportunities to track decision making in realistic environments and show the repercussions of those decisions in a risk-free environment.

Traditionally, simulations have consisted of a single character navigating through scenarios such as flying a plane or making project management decisions. Live simulations incorporate actors playing roles and can be as elaborate as full disaster response training to a terrorist attack. With technology, simulations can also be conducted as group experiences in a classroom, with teams or an individual entering their decisions into a computer as the simulation proceeds. The key to the simulation experience is a debrief discussion afterward when people reflect on their experiences. Simulations not only provide the opportunity to learn from our experiences but also to reflect on our decisions to gain greater insights and improve on what we do.

Out-of-This World Experiences

Virtual immersive environments present truly unique ways to work, think, and learn socially. According to Koreen Olbrish, who has focused exclusively on this space for a decade, immersive environments are most useful when they create an experience that we couldn't otherwise have because of physical or geographical constraints, high expense, or outright danger.[7] Think about experiences you and those in your organization need to have in real life but can't because of some limitation. These experiences are where organizations should start applying the value of virtual immersive environments.

See the Knowledge Around You

Because of the sheer volume of customers it serves, Defense Acquisition University (DAU), part of the U.S. Department of Defense, is building a 3D virtual immersive environment called Nexus, where students will learn acquisition processes through the eyes and locomotion of their avatars. Nexus will run in a browser and give many more people than could ever travel to a physical location access to courses they need for certification.

Mark Oehlert, an anthropologist who works as an innovation evangelist at DAU, is technology advisor for the project. He figures out how to use game technology, simulations, virtual worlds, and other types of social media to create better learning experiences for DAU customers.

He began asking, "What if you, in the person of an avatar, could literally walk through an acquisition process? What if you could change your viewpoint and look at it from a 10,000-foot level or drill deep into it?"

From that seed of an idea, DAU began thinking about creating a spatial way to represent knowledge. It already had communities of practice and knowledge management tools, but what if its new virtual classroom could accrue the wisdom of everybody who passed through it? That classroom would become a knowledge repository where people could access what people who came before them knew and learned. Students could also come back to access it again after class. The class notes there could be built upon, modified, and improved.

Nexus won't replace other forms of e-learning at DAU, but as it improves and more people access it through browsers, it will probably subsume online conference tools because the space is a natural forum for meetings and collaboration. It will also eventually affect the way DAU delivers courses. People at DAU's physical campus will also be able to go into an immersive virtual world to take or augment a class or lesson. They can go there a couple of weeks before a class and see virtual representations of the people they'll be with.[8]

Learning by Doing Complex Work

Researchers have long known that learning by doing is the most effective means of learning certain kinds of things; yet it's often hard to create a safe environment for people to learn new roles on the job. Some scenarios and opportunities are simply too expensive, dangerous, infrequent, or impractical to do in real life. In virtual environments, people can fail safely and create memories that improve performance when recalled later.

Virtual environments, especially simulations and games, have already become an important part of training for emergency responders. A group of trainees can be immersed in a massive simulated airplane crash and then be trained to search for and evacuate survivors, suppress fires, start field triage, and address the media and the FBI. Not only would it take hundreds of person hours and huge expenditures to conduct a live drill of the same magnitude, but there is always the danger of someone getting hurt.

Experts agree simulations can never replace the experience of being surrounded by an actual fire and carrying rescue gear, but these simulations are valuable supplements.

Loyalist College, a mid-size community college 200 kilometers east of Toronto, Canada, uses immersive environments in its Customs Border Services Program.[9] Prior to September 11, 2001, students spent three weeks closely observing a Canadian immigration and

> *Virtual environments, especially simulations and games, have already become an important part of training for emergency responders.*

customs agent on the job. Increased security concerns then prevented people, who were not bonded from working at the border, so on-the-job training was terminated. When students reverted to the classroom for role playing, exercises fell flat. Second Life, the online virtual world, provided a realistic and immersive solution.

Kathryn deGast-Kennedy, coordinator of the program, said, "Even though I have been a Border Services Officer for 28 years, I felt the same level of anxiety in the virtual border crossing as I did 28 years earlier. The virtual experience made me a believer that working within Second Life was as real as it could get." She sees the program expanding into topics such as the anatomy of a motor vehicle search, scans for miniscule yet telltale signs of trouble, and conflict management and dispute resolution.[10]

Loyalist's Customs and Immigration training simulation includes a simplified version of the Thousand Islands, Ontario/Watertown, New York border environment. Some students practice riding across the border as civilians while others play the role of border agents validating identification against records and conducting interviews. A script within the virtual environment generates information from the virtual license plates on the cars passing through the border and displays the information in the guard booth. Certain events are programmed to pop up inside the guard station—just as they might in the real world—such as problem driving records, stolen car warnings, or other red flags. About 5 percent of the license plates are programmed to generate a flag message on the booth monitor, consistent with the statistical probability at real border crossings.

The realistic environment requires students to improvise and think on their feet as they work together—just as they need to do at a real border crossing. "Because it is improv," Ken Hudson, Loyalist's head of Educational Technology, says, "the students have no idea what to expect."[11]

Students who complete the program consistently have a 39 percent higher success rate at testing milestones than those who do not complete work in virtual practice sessions. They also score better grades—roughly 30 percent higher—than their counterparts who receive only classroom training. They excel in giving bilingual greetings, asking mandatory questions, assessing resident status, and exhibiting overall professionalism.

Understanding From Authenticity

Although an avatar is any image that represents a person in an interactive exchange, it does represent an actual human being, and avatars in virtual environments represent many facets of that person. When people interact with other avatars, context can be conveyed and understood through facial expressions, gestures, posture, and position in an environment.

Although many people who promote virtual environments say it's important to make avatars look realistic and reflect to some degree your appearance in the real world, a growing crowd takes an opposing view. One contrarian is Mark Oehlert, the innovation evangelist at DAU, who in real life is a down-to-earth, somewhat intellectual-looking anthropologist. Picture him wearing a photo ID around his neck and a dress shirt.

In Second Life, one of the virtual worlds where Oehlert interacts, he's a seven-foot-tall Celtic warrior named ChuckNorris Mission, who sometimes sports wings and lives in a tiki beach house with an Elvish tower and Roman furniture.

Oehlert explains that his avatar's appearance tells others more about his personality than the way he looks in real life—and he argues that the same is true of everyone's online persona. Common wisdom says that when people have the ability to be anything they want to be or appear to be, you can't trust their representation. He contends that when you remove physical and economic constraints from the way people present themselves, what you may be looking at is actually the truest version of how people see themselves and how they most want others to see them.[12]

At IBM, which has a large presence in Second Life, employees interact as avatars of all types. "You can come to a meeting as a fish," points out Chuck Hamilton, virtual learning leader for the Center for Advanced Learning at IBM, which trains employees across IBM in virtual environments such as Second Life. Hamilton's avatar sports a kilt, a connection to his heritage and the Celtic band he plays with in Vancouver.[13]

Tandem Learning creates 2D and 3D scenario-based simulations that mirror the interactions of pharmaceutical sales representatives interacting with physicians and other healthcare professionals. These simulations allow sales representatives to practice selling and communication skills to ensure they aren't inadvertently violating Food and Drug Administration (FDA) regulations through the language they use to promote their products' use. Other simulations allow sales representatives to view interactions between physicians and patient to better understand how physicians make treatment decisions for their patients. This type of practice provides sales representatives with skill in highly clinical and heavily regulated conversations.[14]

> *What if you could experience first hand the reality of mentally ill people with more compassion and understanding? What if you could feel what it's like to be a person of another gender, color, or nationality?*

Seeing Through Other Eyes, Literally

Psychotherapy helps people change behavior by working to pull people out of themselves—to see their behavior from the perspective of a loved one, for example, or to observe their own thinking habits from a neutral distance.

What if you could experience first hand the reality of mentally ill people with more compassion and understanding? What if you could feel what it's like to be a person of another gender, color, or nationality?

Now, neuroscientists have shown that they can make this experience physical, creating a "body swapping" illusion that could have a profound effect on a range of therapeutic techniques. The brain, when tricked by optical and sensory illusions, can quickly adopt any other human form, no matter how different, as its own.

"You can see the possibilities—putting a male in a female body, young in old, white in black, and vice versa," says Dr. Henrik Ehrsson of the Karolinska Institute in Stockholm, who with his colleague Valeria Petkova has provided grounding for some of the most interesting aspects of what can happen in virtual environments.[15]

Jeremy Bailenson, director of the Virtual Human Interaction Lab at Stanford University, and his colleague Nick Yee call this the *Proteus effect*, after the Greek god who can embody many different self-representations.[16]

In one experiment, the Stanford team found that people agree to contribute more to retirement accounts when they are virtually "age morphed" to look older and that they will exercise more after inhabiting an avatar that works out and loses weight.

Sarah Robbins (aka Intelligal), who teaches at Ball State and is co-author of *Second Life for Dummies*, regularly conducts a cultural awareness experiment with her students. She has them put on giant Kool-Aid pitcher avatars and mill around various Second Life spaces to experience diversity, crowd mentality, exclusion, and discrimination. She explained that because most of her students never felt excluded or discriminated against, the "Kool-Aid man experience" is a way to get them to quickly and easily understand a previously foreign concept. So how did the students react to this new (and strangely unique) exercise? Many of them felt safe because they were in a group of people like themselves. Within five minutes, students learned complex, experiential concepts that are only marginally conveyed during a 50-minute, face-to-face class. Robbins believes these tools can help build a bridge from the place where people are interested and engaged to where they need to go, educationally and in society.[17]

Margaret Regan, president of The FutureWork Institute, creates unique learning experiences for diversity training in virtual immersive environments. Participants "wear" different skin colors and have the opportunity to walk in the shoes—or skin—of another.[18]

There's even a schizophrenia clinic in Second Life, run by psychiatry professors at the University of San Diego, based on longitudinal data of stories from real patients. You can walk into the clinic in Second Life, pick a badge that identifies you as male or female, and within minutes start having hallucinations and hearing voices that murmur in your avatar's ears. As you walk down the hallway, the floor beneath you feels like it's moving a little, like a scene in a Wile E. Coyote cartoon. You pick up a newspaper, and the words get blurry and come to life. Words about psychosis leap out at you.

Play with Possibilities

Often deep learning depends on engaging with materials in realistic environments where you can learn through trial and error. The feel of the experience becomes the basis for understanding how to excel and gain confidence to continue to a higher level.

In a virtual environment you can play any role you like, regardless of who you really are. You can fail in one role, reconnect, and try another one, learning from each.

L'Oréal, the cosmetics company, uses a global recruiting game, Reveal, to bring people up to speed on products and services before they enter the interview process. The skills people learn in virtual environments can be used outside of these spaces too. America's Army, for example, once just a recruiting tool that offers a glimpse of actual army work in a realistic play environment, is now being used as a training tool because it teaches many skills, some at a high level. The U.S. Navy is doing the same thing with its Navy Training Exercise.

Anne Derryberry, analyst and advisor for serious games, online learning games, simulations, and virtual worlds, points out that many of these examples are pre-designed, structured activities leading to a desired result and are often intended for a specific group of people working together online or in the same space.[19] Virtual environments can also give people an opportunity for more serendipitous, less known outcomes when doing complex work.

Whether designed as an environment that mirrors the real world or as a metaphor for the real world, these spaces can also include or be augmented by opportunities for people to debrief and reflect on what they've experienced.

For example, when people at the University of Maryland's Center for Advanced Transportation Technology Laboratory wanted to improve the way traffic incidents are managed in the I-95 corridor, they knew that training and practice were going to be key to interagency coordination. One of the crucial design elements of the virtual incident management training system that was launched was its ability to run a virtual scenario, record the actions of every team member in the training event, and replay the scenario to the group for debrief and critique. With this kind of system, a virtual tractor-trailer crash and gas spill incident on the Maryland–Virginia state line could occur at 3:30 p.m. on a virtual Friday—with no real-world traffic backups of any kind. Any missteps in the handling of the virtual incident can be evaluated, with the added benefit of running a similar virtual incident to practice the corrected activities.

> *Whether designed as an environment that mirrors the real world or as a metaphor for the real world, these spaces can also include or be augmented by opportunities for people to debrief and reflect on what they've experienced.*

Make Time for Serious Play

Byron Reeves, a professor at Stanford, found that the environment a leader works in and learns from has more influence on leadership success than his or her individual traits as a leader. A rich environment, where people can learn to learn and see leadership modeled, can lead to success. Reeves also found that people who may not be high potentials in the real world end up with significant leadership roles in the game environment, which can lead them to seek out leadership opportunities using the skills they have developed online.[20]

IBM uses serious play for learning and work across many lines of business. With more than 3,000 employees involved on two dozen public and private islands in Second Life, a dozen more sites in Active Worlds, and several Open Simulator spaces, IBM has a strong public and private presence in virtual spaces. The company uses these spaces for activities such as collaboration among various research and development teams around the world and experiments on the evolution of user-interface design and how people interact virtually.

Sam Palmisano, Chairman and CEO of IBM, has held worldwide workforce meetings in Second Life, reinforcing the organization's commitment to living its values and creating a strong opportunity for innovation and engagement.

Second Life at IBM is a way to connect across generations and locations. There you'll see very senior IBMers swimming and flying next to people who have been in the business 10 months and others still who have retired and yet are interested in staying connected.

When polled, 85 percent of the people who participated in IBM's Second Life activities reported that mentoring events achieved their objectives and that virtual social spaces were suitable for mentoring and better for connecting with people than a telephone call or a web conference.[21]

Respond to Critics

When you begin talking about and planning a new initiative that involves virtual worlds, you will likely face questions and comments from people who want to temper enthusiasm with caution. Here are the most common objections we hear and ways we believe you can address them.

This All Seems Too Sci-Fi, Too Unreal for My Organization

At some point in history, television was viewed as science fiction. Telephones, computers, and the Internet are all innovations that our ancestors probably never even dreamed of. That does not make them less useful or relevant. Companies that stand the test of time are the ones that recognize the importance of change and innovation when there is a business need.

This Is All Too Expensive

Instructive 2D games can be made relatively cheaply, often from templates that can be updated with the simple insertion of a new audio track. Even developers of powerful 3D games assure us that technology advances will improve efficiencies through scalability, lowering the cost-per-student price. The cost of virtual technologies ranges dramatically from being practically free to requiring significant investments of time, resources, and money.

This Doesn't Create Lasting Change

Underlying every successful virtual immersive environment are sophisticated analytics engines. America's Army is a prime example of how this works. The game uses predictive analytics on data about players' strengths and weaknesses to identify a player's likely response to any new situation, and it adjusts assignments accordingly. Its adaptive nature has big ramifications for play, learning, and work, giving people a genuine opportunity to learn from their mistakes and improve their performance.

It's Not Natural

Although some people find working in a virtual environment unsettling at first, most don't and quickly adapt to the virtual world in the same way we easily integrate into a new city with different smells and sights. Some people choose never to set foot out of their hometown, but most do, and they are likely to enjoy the trip. Virtual immersive environments also offer the opportunity to traverse different planes of reality, something you can't do anywhere else on earth.

No One Will Be Interested

A recent study by the American Society for Training & Development found that although respondents said that virtual world technology is rarely used to a high or very high extent today (4.7 percent of the 743 high-level human resources professionals polled in 2009), the percentage of respondents who indicated it should be used was 24.6.[22] Given how many people don't know the benefits of virtual environments, we suspect this number would be even higher if they understood. How many people complain about the current structure of training or say it could be improved? How many people say training should be more relevant? These environments provide an opportunity to do that.

Recommendations

Get started with a virtual immersive environment by considering what people in your organization would benefit from doing but can't in a healthy, safe, or cost-effective way.

Host a Virtual Meeting with a Captivating Topic

Sometimes enticing people to try something new involves giving them something to do that they already want to do and doing it in a way that will require trying something new in the process. Consider hosting a meeting on a topic your constituents want to know more about (or want to argue about, or couldn't imagine missing) in a virtual environment. Give them plenty of notice and offer mini tutorials on how to get started.

Social interaction improves employee engagement, productivity, and innovation but is often hard to come by in today's far-flung organizations. Once you show immersive environments as training devices, expand them to facilitate collaboration and communication, allowing employees to interact freely without having to be in the same place. Host a big meeting, a worldwide party, or a networking event, or bring in a guest speaker. Make the business case by measuring cost savings and the success of the project.

Create Onramps

Virtual environments are ideal for training and simulations, allowing companies to replicate almost any environment they choose and have employees interact with it, the trainers, and each other. Karl Kapp, professor at Bloomsburg University and co-author of *Learning in 3D*, reminds organizations to "provide participants with an onramp to help them become comfortable with the technology. Time must be allocated in advance of the program to provide basic instruction on navigation. Make mentoring available. Separate the learning associated with coming up to speed in a virtual immersive environment from the experience people will have in the environment itself."[23]

Start at the Very Top or at the Bottom

Someone in a middle management position may have even more fear of presenting new technology ideas than those on the front line. People on the front line are more likely to try something for efficiency's sake and let the results do the selling to the top. Gina Schreck, cofounder and digital immigration officer at Synapse 3Di, often sees the use of immersive technology start in small pockets (sales, project teams, and so forth) of a company; when other groups get wind of the successes, it spreads.[24]

Make It Easy

Even when the cost and efficiency benefits outweigh the business problem, if immersive environments are hard for people to use, they will not adopt them. Recruit volunteers and evangelists to ensure the first experience is positive for people. Offer lots of coaching and flexible time slots to get newcomers oriented and on board.

Show Real Value, not Gimmicks

Joe Miller, vice president of platform and technology development at Linden Lab (operator of Second Life), suggests companies move past simply re-creating real-world training environments, replete with seats, podiums, and screens. "Once the wow factor wears off," he says, "this approach may not be interesting or innovative enough to create a powerful virtual experience."[25]

Mark Oehlert reminds us that even after 10 years of creating e-learning, people still put the "Next" button in the lower right-hand corner of the screen. Virtual immersive environments can (and should) do better than that. Under-engaging, poorly constructed spaces yield little value.[26]

Use the technology to create useful, rather than gimmicky, executions. Use the technology in such a way that it augments even the traditional online experience. Ask yourself, how is this better than just putting these assets online with a more basic tool, loading a video into a media-sharing system, creating a basic e-learning course, or hosting a meeting on a conference bridge?

Consider the opportunity to tear down walls, let people learn through action and interaction, see experiences from angles they never could have in real life, and ask questions that would have been unanswerable in real situations. Virtual immersive environments are far too compelling to miss the opportunity to create something great.

Connecting the Dots
at In-Person Events

"An event should be a happening. If nothing happens then it's just boring. Change the energy. Demonstrate you're after something different. Create something for people to talk about and feel in toes."

—Graham Brown-Martin

Founder, Learning Without Frontiers

◆ ◆ ◆

At The Brewery, a stunning state-of-the-art conference facility in London, the lights were dim but the room was abuzz. The song "Once in a Lifetime" by Talking Heads surrounded everyone like a cloud, making them feel energized, knowing something big was about to begin.

The Handheld Learning Conference delegates chatted, introducing themselves to people they hadn't met before. Some snapped photos, others reported to colleagues at the office, some closed their eyes, taking in the electrified feel of the space.

Graham Brown-Martin, the event producer, stepped to the stage and explained the potent ingredients he had assembled for the following two days. The events he and a handful of others put on are intimate, yet they are growing in size, running rings around larger enterprises because their use of social media has leveled the field.

He shared a story, as he does every year, of his youngest daughter, lovingly referred to as "Handheld Learning Girl." She was born several days before the first Handheld Learning event in 2005, delivered by Brown-Martin at home via instructions on his smartphone because the midwife had not yet arrived. Her development as a person and the technology advancements in those same years offer a timely glimpse of social tool evolution. Thought-provoking talks followed from Malcolm McLaren (former manager of the Sex Pistols), new media literacy professor James Paul Gee, and futurist Ray Kurzweil. News zapped quickly around the twitterverse as delegates tweeted insights from the godfathers respectively of punk, game-based learning, and artificial intelligence. The event began showing up in the list of Twitter's trending topics, and people worldwide joined the conversation.

What might have looked like an ordinary event morphed into a social beehive, punctuated by provocative statements, shared and challenged virally by the community, aggregated and disseminated far and wide.

What might have looked like an ordinary event morphed into a social beehive, punctuated by provocative statements, shared and challenged virally by the community, aggregated and disseminated far and wide. Everything was captured by a small video crew and posted to the event's online community within an hour of each session's end. People sat in corners of the room, blogging and typing quietly, talking and reflecting, considering the implications of the experience on the work they do.

Before the event they had contributed to online communities that would be around for years to come. People who were not at the event could also log in, connect with delegates and speakers, and watch and comment on the posted media.

The coffee and lunch breaks featured food meant to be eaten while talking with others, often with a mobile device in one hand. Asian fusion, cups with lids, all part of the social mix. Evenings typically involved dancing, providing further chances to connect, consider, and fuse learning with life.

Brown-Martin created social media before he curated events. He began as an educational technologist and then joined the entertainment business in music, games, and film. He built a large social networking site aimed at 18 to 34-year-old opinion formers, which streamed radio and video shows, had online editorial pieces for hundreds of thousands of members, and provided a way for them to link.

He realized then that human interaction was vital and arranged still-legendary club nights with the hottest DJs in London and abroad. These were events people came out for, people who had and would continue to connect through his online activities. No advertising was required because everyone was already connected to everyone else.

When he launched a new enterprise, it started as an online professional community, connecting people who otherwise might not have known about one another. He strung together his contacts from the worlds of education, technology, and entertainment in an unusual brew.

It seemed logical to him to bring together people every so often at festivals and conferences that could be recorded and distributed online, enabling the conversation and networking to continue. The events started with social media; that has always driven them, not the other way around.

The Handheld Learning Conference, one of a half dozen he produces on themes such as game-based learning and digital safety, is the world's largest conference on mobile learning. It is also one of the United Kingdom's largest conferences about technology and learning regardless of the platform discussed.

As Brown-Martin reflects on the history of his events, he talks about his naïve expectation that delegates would be largely early adopters and power users. With notable exceptions, most people, while passionately interested in new ways to improve learning, were slower to pick up on the opportunities of social and digital media than Brown-Martin anticipated.

For him the events are a form of activism meant to disrupt the Victorian-style teaching practices living on in the 21st century. There are no badges (using instead music festival–style wrist bracelets), which forces people to talk with one another, introducing themselves in a personal way. There are no conference guides; although it took years, he says, to wean attendees from thinking they needed them. There are still conference bags, but they contain mobile devices—one year a Nintendo DS, another year an iTouch, and in 2010 an iPad.

The conference delivers a heady cocktail, frequently provocative, challenging, polarizing, exhilarating, thought provoking, and exhausting—everything that a good conference ought to be and where participants frequently and in most cases good naturedly are drawn out of traditional comfort zones to confront the new.

Brown-Martin is passionate about learning, innovation, technology, music, and people. His greatest skill, however, has been in spotting trends early and connecting the dots. He doesn't consider himself an event organizer as much as someone who brings together "happenings" that he would like to attend on topics he is passionate about and believes in. He brings about change by using social media to create a platform to see, hear, and engage with those doing remarkable work.

He says, "It's the only way to do it. Social media is the perfect way to connect with the right people, almost like osmosis, creating a venue—and opportunity—where we each can be more."

Growing Together

Coming together to talk, visit, and learn is as old as time. Using in-person opportunities to humanize learning that you've begun (and will continue) online adds a modern dimension.

Saul Kaplan of the Business Innovation Factory, which hosts communities and dialogues focused on what it takes to create transformative change, describes in-person events as a communal Petri dish for growing connections and insights. "Incubation is spontaneous and palpable. It's as if there are luminescent tags networking us together. There is an electric feeling of potential and possibility."[1]

In previous chapters we introduced you to the approaches you can use in your organization to take advantage of the new social learning to extend and deepen collective and individual opportunity to grow in the connected world. People in physical proximity to one another can also use each approach we've covered up to this point.

In this final chapter, we meld the in-person practices we all know with technologies that can enhance the experience in fresh ways. Although our focus is mostly on conferences, many of these practices can be applied to classes and small ad hoc and informal gatherings. We will show how the use of social tools can increase their value, making them remarkable and exhilarating.

Events can mash up the physical and the online worlds. Social networks you already belong to can connect you to people at the event who have interests similar to yours.

This chapter assumes you wear many hats. Sometimes you're a speaker, playing a part akin to a teacher in a classroom, often on a bigger stage. Other times you're an event attendee, a student of sorts, interested in learning all you can. Occasionally you're an event organizer or meeting facilitator, and sometimes you pay the registration fees for your employees, wanting the greatest value for your dollars and their time spent. These events can be conferences put on by professional event producers, corporate events, or gatherings of association members.

In today's connected world, you are probably also an influencer of the work done by those putting on events and who want your business or seek your counsel. Each role provides opportunities to make informed decisions and offer sound advice.

We address how you can take action in each role and then offer a glimpse of some alternative event formats that are beginning to catch on.

Speaker, Teacher, Audience, Student

If you speak often at events, meetings, or classes, you know firsthand that audiences no longer sit quietly absorbing your words and the images you show, waiting to ask a question or make a comment. Technology-enabled societal shifts have started moving the ground under your feet, says Joel Foner, a project manager, process consultant, and blogger, who has engaged large hyper-connected audiences for years.[2] The new social learning, with its emphasis on people learning from one another, plays up the fact that both speakers and attendees have something valuable to share.

Olivia Mitchell, a presentation trainer who writes the "Speaking about Presenting" blog and is considered the leader in tackling thorny issues about presenting in the digital age, says, "There has been a shift in power from the speaker to the audience. The best speakers don't care about themselves, they care about their audience, and they care passionately, working hard to ensure everyone is getting value from their time together."[3]

Through global communication technologies, people now have so much access to each other and to information that they've "grown accustomed to the idea that they can and should be able to discuss, rate, rank, prioritize, link, and converse in text with anyone, at any time," says Foner. "They comment on and rate web sites, blog posts, music, videos, books, vendors, manufacturers—and you and me. Social media everywhere has made this hyper connectedness part of everyday life."

Robert Scoble, a technology evangelist, author, and popular blogger, reminds us that "We're used to living a two-way life online and expect it with an audience, too. Our expectations of speakers and people on stage have changed, for better or for worse."[4]

The Backchannel

Real-time text communication among audience members using something like Twitter or a local chat room during a live event is often referred to as "the backchannel." Backchannel is a term coined in 1970 by linguist Victor Yngve to describe listeners' behaviors during verbal communication. Today the new backchannel represents an audience who is now networked—connected in real time, learning with each other and the world all the time. The backchannel doesn't have a limited number of chairs—anyone can join—and this changes the game for presenters, the audience, and the rest of the world outside the room.

Instead of looking across a sea of faces, you may be speaking to an ocean of heads looking down at their laptops and smartphones, or watching you from behind flipcams connected to people in other rooms and around the world.

When audience members using Twitter add an event hashtag (#) to their tweets, they open the conversation to anyone on Twitter, including those in the room specifically following that tag. For example, #ASTD10 was the hashtag for the 2010 ASTD International Conference, Lotusphere used #LS10 at its 2010 event, and #e2conf is the hashtag used each year for the Enterprise 2.0 conferences. Anyone can run a Twitter search to find all the backchannel tweets related to that event.

A survey of leadership events by production company Weber Shandwick shows that blogging and twittering at conferences has significantly increased in the past few years.[5] The backchannel is increasingly a factor in any sort of education where wifi connections allow people to chitchat, check facts, rate sessions, and evaluate their experiences.

Presenting while people are talking about you can be disconcerting and distracting. In the past, you may have used eye contact with your audience to measure their engagement. Now when you say something brilliant, instead of nods of appreciation, there may be a flurry of thumb tapping. This kind of communication can be terrifying to a speaker because everybody in the room and around the globe participating virtually can now rate you, share their thoughts, comment on your work for better or worse, and point out mistakes—or what they think are mistakes—in the middle of your sentences. For some people, that is "scary beyond measure," adds Foner.

Mitchell says, "To balance that shift, there are huge benefits to individual members of the audience and to the overall output of a conference or meeting. Most of all, it shows people are interested in what you're saying—so interested they want to capture it and share it with others." In her work, Mitchell has identified the following benefits and more.

Real-Time Participation

The backchannel blurs the line between the presenter and the audience and even between those physically in attendance and those participating from afar. Now everyone can participate and share information.

Gary Koelling, founder of Best Buy's BlueShirt Nation, said of a Twitter-fueled meeting, "What struck me was the dynamic of this meeting. It was participatory. No one was talking out loud except the guy presenting. But the conversation was roaring through the room via Twitter. It was exploding. People were asking questions. Pointing out problems. Replying to each other all while the PowerPoint was progressing along its unwaveringly linear path. The contrast couldn't have been more striking. Here are two tools that couldn't be more at odds with each other; the linear, planned, predictable progression of slides versus the raucous, organic free-for-all of Twitter. I wanted the twitterfeed to actually change the presentation—to update it, edit it, extend it, pull it into areas it wasn't exploring."[6]

> *Gary Koelling, founder of Best Buy's BlueShirt Nation, said of a Twitter-fueled meeting, "What struck me was the dynamic of this meeting. It was participatory. No one was talking out loud except the guy presenting. But the conversation was roaring through the room via Twitter."*

Real-Time Focus

"Prior to the technology advancements, I backchanneled with myself," notes Dean Shareski, a digital learning consultant. "That is, I processed by thinking or taking notes. I would ask questions and answer them myself. The more engaging a speaker, the less I backchannel. That said, some less engaging speakers who understand and permit back channeling can create as powerful a learning experience as the most dynamic speaker. The more the presentation relies on the backchannel, the more I focus. Knowing that my comments are going to be seen by the presenter or live participants seems to make me pay more attention. The more I'm allowed to interact and play with the content, the more I'm engaged and ultimately the more I learn."[7]

Online community maven Rachel Happe likes that Twitter enables her to participate in presentations without disrupting them. Happe says, "Twitter allows me to add my perspective to what is being presented and that keeps me more engaged than just sitting and listening—even if no one reads it."[8]

Real-Time Innovation

As your presentation sparks ideas, audience members can tweet them and build on one another's thoughts. They can build and share their own insight into what's being discussed.

As a speaker, if you monitor the backchannel, you can innovate along with the audience. Jeffrey Veen, designer, author, and entrepreneur, was moderating a panel at a conference and monitoring the backchannel through his smartphone. "As the conversation on stage continued, the stream of questions and comments from the audience intensified. I changed my tactics based on what I saw. I asked questions the audience was asking, and I immediately felt the tenor of the room shift in my favor. It felt a bit like cheating on an exam."[9]

Real-Time Contribution

People tweeting during presentations add explanations, elaborations, and useful links related to the content. "My 'take-away content' from the backchannel equaled or surpassed what I got from presentations directly," said Liz Lawley, director of the lab for social computing at the Rochester Institute of Technology. "I can already see that there's more I want to go back to and digest, discuss, and extend."[10]

Instead of asking your neighbor, "What did she mean by that?" you can tweet your question to the group, and someone will tweet back an opinion. Laura Fitton, entrepreneur and founder of Twitter-store oneforty, recounts a time when some of her colleagues who'd helped with the presentation were following the event virtually and were answering questions asked by those in the audience as she gave her talk.[11]

Remote or on stage, Bryan Mason, co-founder of Small Batch, calls this person an "ombudsman for the audience." At an event he and Jeff Veen hosted, they put a desk on stage and had a friend sit right there keeping tabs on Twitter, an instant message tool, and email, listening to what people were talking about. She synthesized the questions and sprinkled them into the conversation in real time.[12]

Real-Time Connections

Being at a conference where you don't know anyone can be intimidating. People who know each other cluster together, and you can feel out of the action. But if you participate in the backchannel, you get to know people virtually and can then introduce yourself in person at the next break.

Real-Time Evaluation

With a backchannel you get immediate feedback when you search the event's #hashtag and the speaker's name and presentation keywords.

Paul Gillin, author of *Secrets of Social Media Marketing* and *The New Influencers,* remembers years ago waiting six months to get audience evaluations, so the immediacy of tweeted feedback is wonderful for him. He also uses it to get a quick read on the tech savviness of the audience and adjusts accordingl.[13]

Graham Brown-Martin knows an event is working well when he receives ample feedback, even when people snipe about the coffee or the price of London beer. He reposts all comments to an online community. It's part of the personality of his organization to encourage and publish commentary, even if it's outrageously negative. Asked why, he responds, "Because they can be so funny!" He adds that feedback can be helpful in seeing situations from others' vantage points.[14]

Takeaway

We've all been to events where good ideas are hatched and projects are planned, but often, despite the best intentions, things lose steam after the event is over and nothing much gets done. Can we—should we—really rely on just our brains and notes to gain value from events?

Even the best presentations have limited value if you can't revisit their best content as you reflect on what you experienced. New digital tools can support such access.

These include just-in-time book publishing, tweetbooks, live blogging, and live video blogging.

Publish a Book

Just-in-time book publishing is a way for anyone to create and publish a book. Event organizers can produce such books compiled from content created by speakers and attendees. Pepper the book with observations from people walking the event, doing interviews, taking polls, and snapping photos.

Great Conference Websites

Encourage conference producers to include the following on their event websites, all updated frequently:

- an attendee list, with links to participants' websites and Twitter feeds
- a schedule, updated regularly, with changes noted
- Twitter posts from the event, organized by RSS feed from the #hashtag; can also have a stream of tweets from the official event Twitter account
- a Facebook fan box linking to the event's Facebook page
- a Flickr badge and links to tagged photos and videos; flipcharts and graphs can be scanned or photographed throughout the event, then posted to Flickr and to the website
- a video feed of sessions fed live into the site, then archived
- a link to YouTube search results tagged with the event's hashtag
- a place where an audio feed can be added in real time and where podcasts of sessions can be made available later
- links to blogs of those attendees writing about the event
- a wiki, online community, or content management system where delegates can post notes from event sessions
- an RSS feed for tracking changes to all of the above
- speaker biographies with links to their websites and Twitter feeds
- local information for parking, mass transit, local restaurants, hospitals, and museums.

The books can be sold online and delivered in hard copy. Events including PopTech, Maker Faire, and Web 2.0 Conference create their own books, sometimes from the main stage, giving participants a different medium to learn from over time.

Create a Tweetbook

Usually made up of the tweets from an event, Tweetbooks create a narrative of what people noticed, attended to, commented on, and shared. Trish Uhl, learning strategist and founder of Owl's Ledge, describes a

Tweetbook as a compilation of historical tweets documenting a trend, news story, or event as reported from the twitterverse.[15] At the eLearning Guild's 2009 conference, attendee and education technology specialist Tracy Hamilton took on the task of creating the event's Tweetbook. It included more than 5,100 tweets chronicling the preconference events, general and concurrent sessions, and an alternative reality game run during the conference.[16]

Live Blogging

Live bloggers transcribe or create commentary about an event as it unfolds. The blogs encourage real-time commentary from readers—either from other participants in the room, people who are at the event but in another room, or people who are participating virtually—which can be brought back into the event to build even more ideas and perspectives.

Bloggers may use conventional blog tools or, for large-scale events involving many bloggers, opt for tools specifically designed for live blogging. Live blogging platforms provide the ability to integrate images, audio files, video clips, presentation slide decks, and other multimedia content, enabling feedback and participation with the blog stream.

Live Video Blogging

Taking live blogging a step further, live video blogging enables bloggers to send live, real-time video streams to the web during events. With live video blogging, web viewers can see and hear the event as it happens, and those at the event can have a record of everything that happened. Real-time video broadcasting used to require renting an expensive mobile video truck. Today, a handheld video camera, a webcam attached to a notebook computer, or a smartphone that supports live video streaming can show thousands of people across the world the event as it happens and go viral with the event's tweets and blog posts.

Because the stream can be recorded, after the event it can also be indexed and made part of a media-sharing site or online community along with videos captured but not streamed by event participants.

Together these videos can convey a message and generate conversation that can lead to more learning and change.

Respond to Critics

As with all new and atypical ideas, there will be resisters. Here are the most common objections we hear and ways we believe you can address them.

People Aren't Paying Attention

People who appear to be fully engaged with their smartphones and laptops may still be paying attention to you—even more so than if they are looking at you. But if you think you'll do a better job if people are looking at you, consider opening your presentation this way: "I notice many of you are using your phones and laptops. I'm absolutely fine with that. But I also know that I can do a better job if you are engaging with me and looking at me. So when you're not using your phones and laptops I'd love it if you can look up."

> *Many people still assume that someone who appears to be doing something other than listening to a presenter cannot be learning what the presenter is covering. This assumption, however, is not supported by evidence.*

Scott Berkun in his book, *Confessions of a Public Speaker*, describes an approach he's taken. He says to his audience, "Here's a deal. I'd like you to give me your undivided attention for five minutes. If after five minutes you're bored, you think I'm an idiot, or you'd rather browse the web than listen, you're free to do so. In fact, I won't mind if you get up and leave after five minutes. But for the first 300 seconds, please give me your undivided attention."[17] Most people close their laptops and put their smartphones away.

Another approach is to put your Twitter ID on your first slide and then ask who in the room is currently on Twitter, a social networking site, or is live blogging. When you see their hands you know who is probably writing about you and not ignoring you.

Chapter 7

People Cannot Learn from Me and Social Media Simultaneously

Many people still assume that someone who appears to be doing something other than listening to a presenter cannot be learning what the presenter is covering. This assumption, however, is not supported by evidence.

Many people use secondary tasks to help them stay engaged and focused. In an experiment reported in *Applied Cognitive Psychology*, doodlers were able to recall 29 percent more details from a phone conversation than non-doodlers, for instance.[18]

Researchers believe that by using slightly more mental resources, doodling helps prevent the mind from wandering. This study is part of an emerging recognition in psychology that secondary tasks aren't always a distraction from primary tasks but can sometimes actually be beneficial.

Edie Eckman, fiber arts educator and author of *How to Knit* and *The Crochet Answer Book* and a frequent speaker at conferences, points out that when she speaks to people who are knitting and crocheting, she sees laser-like focus. It's as if the handwork allows them to connect with other people far better than if they were empty handed.[19]

The secondary tasks we use to stay focused are now often high tech. People can take notes on their smartphones and laptops, or they may have a game on their phone equivalent to doodling. Seeing a tweet can reinforce what's going on in the session or introduce peripheral topics that will expand the attendees' thinking. Taking notes in an online community can offer useful detail to others back at the office and provide a springboard for further conversation when returning to work.

Recommendations

We opened with the story of the Handheld Learning Conference because it was a natural setting for combining the benefits of mobile technology and the joy we get from connecting with people in person in real time. Graham Brown-Martin points out, however, that the first few years of the London-based event weren't all that interesting.

It took hours of culling suggestions from previous event attendees for the next years' events to capture the right mix. The event brought together more than 1,500 delegates from around the world plus more than 200 young learners who had been sponsored by various schools and programs.

In addition to those who physically joined the conference, the event appeared as a trend for three consecutive days in the global top 10 on Twitter, demonstrating how far this movement and its participants reached.

As we spoke with Brown-Martin and others who are spurring on the new social learning at in-person events, we found the following themes.

Don't Go Unless There's Time to Share a Meal

People may open up more when sharing a good meal. If you only have time for one short day of people talking at you, consider ways you can learn from them online instead. So far, there's no way to duplicate online that emotional connection—the *joie de vivre*, the juice, the joy of life—we share in person.

Trust One Another

To attend an event involves sacrifice. People come together because they are committed to getting something valuable from the event. When organizers trust attendees and speakers to determine for themselves what patterns are relevant, what connections are valuable, and which stories are most energizing, events are more likely to be memorable. Although it seems basic, our nature is to be prescriptive, to tell people what they are supposed to get out of an event, what conclusions they are supposed to reach, who they should collaborate with, and what they should work on. If you trust the audience to create the insights and connections that make sense to them and you provide an environment that is conducive to connecting, the magic will happen.

Prepare Yourself

If you choose to go to an in-person event, prepare yourself beforehand by learning as much as you can about what the event offers. Kaliya Hamlin, at the forefront of the unconference movement, encourages people to identify questions you want to ask and topics you want to learn more about.[20] Here are more suggestions for preparing:

- To prepare to visit trade show booths, type keywords about your industry niche into your favorite search engine and see what suppliers come up. Visit the websites of the companies that will be demonstrating their wares. Figure out which suppliers you want to meet and talk with.

- To prepare for the content of the event, read papers and articles posted to the event's website before you go. See if speakers have posted slide decks from previous conferences on Slideshare and look through them.

- To get a sense of speakers' styles, whenever you can, watch them on YouTube or see if they include video clips on their own websites.

- Get a sense of who will be there by reading the blogs and viewing the Flickr streams of speakers and anyone you know will be attending.

Face time with other people is valuable, rare, and expensive. Have meaningful conversations, get advice from peers, and tackle challenging issues in ways that you don't feel you could do online.

Get Twitter-Ready

If the conference doesn't provide it, give your presentation a Twitter hashtag. Make it as short as possible so people can include it on every tweet. Make it unique so people outside your audience don't accidentally use it.

Encourage people to get the conversation going ahead of time by using the hashtag that you developed. Their questions may reveal themes you will want to cover in the presentation.

Stream and display the Twitter backchannel on a screen behind you that everyone (including you) can see and ask people to tweet their questions and comments. Spend time at the beginning of your presentation explaining how you will respond to the Twitter stream, and you'll find audience members will be more likely to use it responsibly rather than tweet things like "Hi Mom."

Ask a colleague or a volunteer from the audience to monitor the feed and interrupt you if any questions or comments need to be addressed right away. If you can't find someone to take on this role, take regular breaks to check Twitter. You can combine this with asking the audience for "out-loud" questions too.

Invite people to use the hashtag after the session, posing additional questions and tapping into the collective experience of others who participated in person or virtually.

Set a Mood

Consider all of the conditions that enhance a social atmosphere: time to talk with people, comfortable seating and lighting, and even good music. Lotusphere 2010, with more than 8,000 people, opened with two street violinists, Nuttin But Strings, and a drummer getting everyone pumped up. People tweeted, downloaded files from the website, ordered CDs, and talked to those around them while they listened. This created an energetic vibe that said, "Get ready for something great." As a speaker, consider adding music to your presentation, providing time for people to talk with one another, and thinking about the environment you're creating where people are excited to learn.

Afterword

◆ ◆ ◆

Now what?

Social media has arrived, regardless of your participation. People are social and will connect with the new technologies. You have two choices for involvement—get in the way or get on board.

Harnessing social media to facilitate the new social learning in the organization has only just begun. It takes intention to create a culture where learning is part of the fabric, core values, and infrastructure. Sure, we can learn by bumping into the obstacles we encounter in our work. Sure, people can and will learn when they must. However, the cultural shift that occurs when social learning is designed into the work process is life changing. It doesn't just add new tasks to your workload. It literally changes the way the whole company learns, works, and succeeds.

Once you move away from the push of information to the pull of learning, you liberate creative powers in your people to succeed in this rapidly changing environment. Once you make it easy for people to inquire and announce activities and projects and you create an environment where people are not afraid to fail, you allow them to ask the really hard questions. And you begin to get answers you never could have found otherwise.

In a simpler world, what we needed to know to do our jobs well was reasonably well defined. It made sense to broadcast both orders and information from the top down. These days, it's not so easy. We have more information, more stakeholders, and more complexities. And we have less time to train. Learning research is quite clear about this: The more engaged people are, the more effectively they learn. In other words, the more questions they ask, the stronger their learning process becomes. Social learning is about making it easier for people to find both their questions and their voice.

We are not a passive blank slate or an empty cup waiting to be filled with wisdom. We are meaning-seeking creatures. Constructing an understanding based on what we find important is proving to be a far richer and more productive model for learning. The theory of knowledge called social constructivism—that reality is constructed by people acting on their interpretations and knowledge of it—is proving to be quite useful.

The challenge of the modern organization is no longer how we can simply beat the competition. We now have to look at issues of sustainability and take a global perspective. We need to attend not only to planetary survival but also to the vitality of whole industries and financial markets. Frankly, we can no longer just sit alone and come up with grand solutions that will work seamlessly across industries, across generations, and across innovations. Our world has simultaneously become too complex and too small to do that.

What we need are new ways to make sense of the mountain of information coming in our direction. We need new ways to filter content, to save information, and to pose questions to trusted sources. What we need is a more complete way to learn. It is our hope that the new social learning we have begun to identify in this book will take us all in that direction.

Amazing things are happening with collaborations that only a few years ago would have been impossible. We have pointed out pockets of excellence in disparate places, from the Mayo Clinic to Chevron to the CIA. And we made suggestions for how you might proceed.

Remember, though: Social learning is not just about being social. It's not just a matter of having the right tools. It's about making learning a priority and using the tools of social media to facilitate a culture where we get better at getting better. It's no longer about just being a better competitor. It's now about being a stronger contributor and a savvier learner.

We walked a fine line in this book between being alarmist and simply expressing our excitement about the radical changes occurring. We have given countless action steps you can take. But it was never our intention to overwhelm. The great thing about the new social learning is that you can start small. There is no need for mass adoption, for total buy-in, or for group consensus. It doesn't have to be done the same way others do it. Once you begin to ask the big questions, a workable model will arise. All you need is the courage to begin the journey. It might be as simple as noticing where social learning is already working in your organization and asking what you can do to improve on that.

Start from where you are. Do what you can. Ask for help. And enjoy the ride. It has been an honor to take you on this journey. We hope the journey of social learning transforms you and those you serve.

Appendix: Governance

♦ ♦ ♦

Organizations considering deploying social software for communication and learning are often concerned with how to govern its use. Should they be heavy-handed in their policies or trust people to use common sense? The most effective policies we've seen fall somewhere in between: comprehensive and educational, using the guidelines to coach employees through how they are expected to behave online and treating people as trustworthy.

> Chris Boudreaux, an executive at Converseon, created SocialMediaGovernance .com, a site full of tools and resources to help managers and leaders with social applications. The policies page on this site provides examples of social media guidelines, policies, and templates from organizations of all sizes in the public and private sectors.

An exemplar in social media governance is IBM, whose official guidelines aim to provide helpful, practical advice—and also to protect both IBM employees and IBM itself, as the company embraces social computing. The guidelines were created by IBMers collaborating with one another using an internal wiki and have evolved several times since first established in 2005 as new technologies and social networking tools become available.

They begin with a request to those reading the guidelines: "Have you seen social computing behavior or content that is not in keeping with these guidelines? Report inappropriate content via email" (which is sent to a content administrator who looks into the report).

The retail giant Nordstrom provides social networking guidelines for its employees to help them dialogue and connect with current and future customers and with each other. The company explains that these guidelines are intended to help employees understand how to "share thoughts, views, and perspectives—as a Nordstrom representative—in the virtual world." Additional detail for each guideline is provided on the company's website—organized under six main headings:

♦ Use good judgment.

♦ Be respectful.

♦ Be transparent.

♦ Be humble.

♦ Be human.

♦ Be a good listener.

In addition, the company asks employees *not* to share

♦ confidential information

♦ private and personal information—yours', customers', and co-workers'.

With an estimated 5,000 conversations per day about the company on social media outlets, The Coca-Cola Company provides its Online Social Media Principles on its website "to help empower our associates to participate in this new frontier of marketing and communications, represent our Company, and share the optimistic and positive spirits of our brands."

The company explains that these principles are intended to outline how the company's shared values should be demonstrated in the social media space and encourages its employees (referred to as associates) to explore and engage in social media communities at a level in which they feel comfortable. The company advises associates to "have fun, but be smart" and to "use sound judgment and common sense" in online worlds just as you would do in the physical world.

IBM Social Computing Guidelines: Blogs, Wikis, Social Networks, Virtual Worlds, and Social Media

Responsible Engagement in Innovation and Dialogue

Whether or not an IBMer chooses to create or participate in a blog, wiki, online social network, or any other form of online publishing or discussion is his or her own decision. However, emerging online collaboration platforms are fundamentally changing the way IBMers work and engage with each other, clients, and partners.

IBM is increasingly exploring how online discourse through social computing can empower IBMers as global professionals, innovators, and citizens. These individual interactions represent a new model: not mass communications, but masses of communicators.

Therefore, it is very much in IBM's interest—and, we believe, in each IBMer's own—to be aware of and participate in this sphere of information, interaction, and idea exchange:

To learn: As an innovation-based company, we believe in the importance of open exchange and learning—between IBM and its clients and among the many constituents of our emerging business and societal ecosystem. The rapidly growing phenomenon of user-generated web content—blogging, social web applications, and networking—are emerging important arenas for that kind of engagement and learning.

To contribute: IBM—as a business, as an innovator, and as a corporate citizen—makes important contributions to the world, to the future of business and technology, and to public dialogue on a broad range of societal issues. As our business activities increasingly focus on the provision of transformational insight and high-value innovation—whether to business clients or those in the public, educational, or health sectors—it becomes increasingly important for IBM and IBMers to share with the world the exciting things we're learning and doing and to learn from others.

In 1997, IBM recommended that its employees get out onto the Internet—at a time when many companies were seeking to restrict their employees' Internet access. In 2005, the company made a strategic decision to embrace the blogosphere and to encourage IBMers to participate. We continue to advocate IBMers' responsible involvement today in this rapidly growing space of relationship, learning, and collaboration.

Source: Excerpted from the introduction to *IBM's Social Computing Guidelines;* for full guidelines, see www.ibm.com/blogs/zz/en/guidelines.html.

In addition to describing the expectations for associates' behavior in online social media communities and the expectations and 10 principles for online spokespeople, Coke's Online Social Media Principles also describe five core values for engaging in online social media communities:

♦ **Transparency** in every social media engagement

♦ **Protection** of consumers' privacy

♦ **Respect** of copyrights, trademarks, rights, and other third-party rights, including user-generated content

♦ **Responsibility** in the use of technology

♦ **Utilization** of best practices and compliance with regulations to ensure the principles reflect appropriate standards of behavior

For more details on Coke's social media principles and those of the other organizations presented here, visit:

♦ **Coke's Online Social Media Principles:**
www.thecoca-colacompany.com/socialmedia/

♦ **Converseon:**
SocialMediaGovernance.com

♦ **IBM Social Computing Guidelines:**
www.ibm.com/blogs/zz/en/guidelines.html

♦ **Nordstrom Social Networking Guidelines:**
about.nordstrom.com/help/our-policies/social-media
-guidelines.asp

Notes and Resources

Notes

Chapter 1

[1] C. Brogan and J. Smith, *Trust Agents: Using the Web to Build Influence, Improve Reputation, and Earn Trust* (Hoboken, NJ: John Wiley & Sons, 2009).

[2] C. Shirky, "Keynote address on social software at the O'Reilly Emerging Technology Conference, Santa Clara, CA, April 24, 2003, retrieved June 17, 2010 at http://www.shirky.com/writings/group_enemy.html.

[3] S. Boyd, Interview with authors, 2009.

[4] For more on social learning theory, see B. Elkjaer, "Social Learning Theory: Learning as Participation in Social Processes," in *The Blackwell Handbook for Organizational Learning and Knowledge Management*, ed. M. Easterby-Smith and M. A. Lyles (Malden, MA: Wiley-Blackwell, 2003).

[5] A. Bandura, *Social Learning Theory* (Upper Saddle River, NJ: Prentice Hall, 1977).

[6] J. Piaget, *Psychology of Intelligence*, Routledge Classics, trans. M. Piercy and D.E. Berlyne (London: Routledge, 2001).

[7] P. Berger and T. Luckman, *The Social Construction of Reality: The Treatise in the Sociology of Knowledge* (London: Penguin, 1967).

[8] V. Landau, E. Clegg, and D. Engelbart, *The Engelbart Hypothesis: Dialogs with Douglas Engelbart*, 2d ed. (Berkeley, CA: Next Press, 2009).

[9] ASTD (American Society for Training & Development), *The Rise of Social Media: Enhancing Collaboration and Productivity Across Generations*, Research Report (Alexandria, VA: ASTD Press, 2010).

[10] For more on women's use of social media, see She's Connected Multimedia Corporation, "The Power of Social Networking for Women: A Compilation of Primary and Secondary Research," 2009, retrieved June 21, 2010 at http://shesconnectedmultimedia.com/pdf/report.pdf.

[11] W. Hodgins, "The Snowflake Effect: The Future of Mashups and Learning, "Becta Emerging Technologies Report, 2009, retrieved June 17, 2010 at http://emergingtechnologies.becta.org.uk/index .php?rid=14146.

[12] A. Toffler, *The Third Wave* (New York: Bantam Books, 1980).

[13] T.L. Friedman, *The World Is Flat: A Brief History of the Twenty-First Century*, 3d ed. (New York: Picador, 2007).

[14] B. Picciano, Interview, 2009.

[15] C. Li, *Open Leadership: How Social Technology Can Transform the Way You Lead* (San Francisco: Jossey-Bass, 2010).

[16] The 70/20/10 learning concept was developed by Morgan McCall, Robert W. Eichinger, and Michael M. Lombardo at the Center for Creative Leadership and is specifically mentioned in *The Career Architect Development Planner*, 3rd edition, by Michael M. Lombardo and Robert W. Eichinger. It is adopted by Princeton University as part of their Learning Philosophy. For more information, see http://en.wikipedia.org/wiki/70/20/10_ Model and http://www.princeton.edu/hr/learning/philosophy/.

[17] E. Wenger, http://www.ewenger.com.

[18] elearningcoach, "Informal Learning: An Interview with Jay Cross," retrieved June 18, 2010 at http://theelearningcoach.com/ elearning2-0/informal-learning-an-interview-with-jay-cross/.

[19] M.J. Rosenberg, Interview with Pat Galagan, 2009.

[20] H. Jarche, "Work Is Learning, Learning Work," 2009, retrieved June 18, 2010 at http://www.jarche.com/2009/05/work-is-learning -learning-work/.

[21] H. Rheingold, *The Virtual Community: Homesteading on the Electronic Frontier*, rev. ed. (Cambridge, MA: MIT Press, 2000).

[22] J. Surowiecki, *The Wisdom of the Crowds: Why Many Are Smarter Than the Few and How Collective Wisdom Shapes Business, Economies, Societies, and Nations* (New York: Little, Brown, 2004).

[23] E. Wagner, Interview with authors, 2009.

[24] A. Rossett, Interview with authors, 2009.

[25] C. Rasmussen, Interview with authors, 2009.

[26] G. Fowler, Interview with authors, 2009.

Chapter 2

[1] P. Romeo, Interview with authors, 2009.

[2] W.S. Smith, *Decoding Generational Differences: Fact, Fiction…Or Should We Just Get Back to Work?* Deloitte Development LLC, 2008, retrieved July 22, 2010 at http://www.deloitte.com/assets/Dcom-UnitedStates/Local%20Assets/Documents/us_Talent_DecodingGenerational Differences.pdf.

[3] Quote from blog in Chet Wood's D Street profile.

[4] R. Happe, Interview with authors, 2009.

[5] For more information about The Community Value Project see http://domino.research.ibm.com/cambridge/research.nsf/99751d8eb5 a20c1f852568db004efc90/47d70b4f5634346685256e200067b05a?Ope nDocument and www.crossanalytics.com.

[6] To learn more EMC's internal online community, see http://jamiepappas.typepad.com.

[7] D. Cohen and L. Prusak, *In Good Company: How Social Capital Makes Organizations Work* (Boston: Harvard Business Press, 1991).

[8] R.J. Light, *Making the Most of College: Students Speak Their Minds* (Cambridge, MA: Harvard University Press, 2001).

[9] W.S. Smith, *Decoding Generational Differences.*

[10] S. Silverthorn, "Understanding Users of Social Networks," September 14, 2009, retrieved July 22, 2010, at http://hbswk.hbs.edu/item/6156.html.

[11] P. Galagan, "Letting Go," *T+D,* September 2009.

[12] R. Merrifield, *Rethink: A Business Manifesto for Cutting Costs and Boosting Innovation* (Upper Saddle River, NJ: Pearson, 2009).

[13] C. Thompson, "Brave New World of Digital Intimacy," *The New York Times,* September 5, 2008.

[14] C. Shirky, "A Speculative Post on the Idea of Algorithmic Authority," 2009, retrieved June 18, 2010 at http://www.shirky.com/weblog/2009/11/a-speculative-post-on-the-idea-of-algorithmic-authority/.

[15] P. Thornton, Interview with authors, 2009.

[16] Booz Allen Hamilton, "Employees Connect, Contribute on Enterprise 2.0 Portal," 2009, retrieved June 18, 2010 at http://www.boozallen.com/about/article_news-ideas/42033790.

[17] G. Koelling, Interview with authors, 2009.

[18] L. Fitton, Interview with authors, 2009.

[19] C. Figallo, *Hosting Web Communities: Building Relationships, Increasing Customer Loyalty, and Maintaining A Competitive Edge* (Hoboken, NJ: John Wiley & Sons, 1998).

[20] IBM, "Pfizer's 'Idea Farm' Harvest Innovative Solutions to Business Problems," Case Study, 2009, retrieved June 18, 2010 at http://www-01.ibm.com/software/success/cssdb.nsf/CS/CCLE-7VC3CY?OpenDocument&Site=default&cty=en_us.

[21] A. Adamson, "Companies Should Encourage Social Networking Among Employees," 2009, retrieved June 18, 2010 at http://www.forbes.com/2009/06/02/charles-schwab-spy-facebook-leadership-cmo-network-adamson.html.

[22] Society for New Communication Research, Beeline Research, and Deloitte, "The Tribalization of Business," 2009, retrieved June 18, 2010 at http://www.tribalizationofbusiness.com.

[23] J. Bancroft, Interview with authors, 2009.

[24] J. Pappas, Interview with authors, 2009.

[25] J. Walton, Interview with authors, 2009.

[26] B. Kaliski, Interview with authors, 2009.

Chapter 3

[1] D. Pontefract, Interview with authors, 2009.

[2] T. Vander Wal, "Folksonomy Coinage and Definition," 2007, retrieved June 21, 2010 at http://vanderwal.net/folksonomy.html.

[3] T. Davenport and J. Beck, *The Attention Economy: Understanding the New Currency of Business* (Boston: Harvard Business School Press, 2001).

[4] Accordent, "Marathon Oil Corporation Taps Rich Vein of Streaming Media Content for Educating and Communicating with Its Global Workforce," Case Study, retrieved June 18, 2010 at http://www.accordent.com/documents/caseStudies/marathon.pdf.

[5] T. Starner, "Video Nation," *Human Resource Executive Online,* 2007, retrieved June 18, 2010 at http://www.hreonline.com/HRE/story.jsp?storyId=33267457.

Chapter 4

[1] M. Flinsch, Interview with authors, 2009.

[2] E. Turner, Interview with authors, 2009.

[3] A. Silvers, Interview with authors, 2009.

[4] D. Wilkins, Interview with authors, 2009.

[5] D. Pogue, "Twittering Tips for Beginners," Pogue's Posts, January 15, 2009, retrieved July 22, 2010 at http://pogue.blogs.nytimes.com/2009/01/15/twittering-tips-for-beginners/?pagemode=print.

[6] B. Betts, Interview with authors, 2009.

[7] G. Hegenbart, Interview with authors, 2009.

[8] F. LeGendre, Interview with authors, 2009.

[9] M. Mohan and T. Stone, Interview with authors, 2009.

[10] J. Hart, Interview with authors, 2009.

[11] M. Lentz, Interview with authors, 2009.

[12] G. Minks, Interview with authors, 2009.

[13] C. Miro, Interview with authors, 2009.

[14] B. Picciano, Interview, 2009.

[15] These examples of how government has been using Twitter are cited in S. Israel, *Twitterville: How Businesses Can Thrive in the New Global Economy* (New York: Portfolio, 2009).

[16] K. Forrister, Interview with authors, 2009.

[17] D. Cathy, Interview with authors, 2009.

[18] B. Ives, Interview with authors, 2009.

[19] J. Dorsey, "Jack Dorsey Presents Twitter," May 30, 2008, retrieved July 22, 2010 at http://www.vimeo.com/1094070?pg=embed&sec=1094070.

Chapter 5

[1] S. Dennehy, Interview with authors, 2009.

[2] D.C. Andrus, "The Wiki and the Blog: Toward a Complex Adaptive Intelligence Community," *Studies in Intelligence* 49(3), retrieved June 20, 2010 at http://ssrn.com/abstract=755904.

[3] D. Burke, Interview with authors, 2009.

[4] M. Calabresi, "Wikipedia for Spies: The CIA Discovers Web 2.0.," *Time,* April 8, 2009, retrieved June 20, 2010 at http://www.time.com/time/nation/article/0,8599,1890084,00.html.

[5] A. Levin, "BookBlog," 2009, retrieved June 20, 2010 at http://www.alevin.com/?m=200909.

[6] V. Landau, E. Clegg, and D. Engelbart. *The Engelbart Hypothesis: Dialogs with Douglas Engelbart,* 2d ed. (Berkeley, CA: Next Press, 2009).

[7] M. Eggebrecht, "Social Networking Takes Flight at NASA," 2009, retrieved June 20, 2010 at http://www.ciozone.com/index.php/Case -Studies/Social-Networking-Takes-Flight-at-NASA.html.

[8] A. Andersson, Interview with authors, 2009.

[9] *T+D.* "Igniting a Passion for Learning," October 2008: 42-4.

[10] J. Sullivan, Interview with authors, 2009.

[11] R. Ruffolo, "IBM Uses Wiki Approach to Corporate Training," *IT World Canada,* November 19, 2008, retrieved June 20, 2010 at http://www.itworld canada.com/news/ibm-uses-wiki-approach-to-corporate-training/06056.

[12] S. Mader, *Wikipatterns* (Indianapolis, IN: John Wiley & Sons, 2008).

[13] E.E. Kim, Interview with authors, 2009.

Chapter 6

[1] K. Renner, Interview with authors, 2009.

[2] K. Olbrish, Interview with authors, 2009.

[3] E. Driver, "Immersive Internet," 2008, retrieved June 20, 2010 at http://www.thinkbalm.com/immersive-internet/.

[4] D. Thomas and J. Seely Brown, "Learning for a World of Constant Change: Homo Sapiens, Homo Faber & Homo Ludens Revisited," in *University Research for Innovation (Glion Colloquium Series),* ed. L. Weber and J. Duderstadt (Hoboken, NJ: Wiley Economica, 2010).

[5] K. Kapp and T. O'Driscoll, *Learning in 3D: Adding a New Dimension to Enterprise Learning and Collaboration* (San Francisco: Pfeiffer, 2010).

[6] For more on simulations, see C. Quinn, *Engaging Learning: Designing e-Learning Simulation Games* (San Francisco: Pfeiffer, 2005).

[7] Olbrish, Interview.

[8] M. Oehlert, Interview with authors, 2009.

[9] For a full case study of Loyalist College's program, see Linden Research Inc., "Virtual World Simulation Prepares Real Guards on the U.S.-Canadian Border: Loyalist College in Second Life," Case Study (San Francisco: Linden Research Inc., 2009), retrieved July 13, 2010 at http://secondlifegrid.net.s3.amazonaws.com/docs/Second_Life_Case_Loyalist_EN.pdf.

[10] Linden Research Inc., "Virtual World Simulation."

[11] Linden Research Inc., "Virtual World Simulation."

[12] Oehlert, Interview.

[13] C. Hamilton, Interview with authors, 2009.

[14] Olbrish, Interview.

[15] B. Carey, "Standing in Someone Else's Shoes, Almost for Real," *The New York Times,* December 1, 2008, retrieved June 20, 2010 at http://www.nytimes.com/2008/12/02/health/02mind.html.

[16] Carey, Standing in Someone Else's Shoes.

[17] Synapse 3Di. "3D Training Learning Collaboration: A Virtual Worlds Conference LIVE from DC," Conference notes, 2009, retrieved June 20, 2010 at http://ja-jp.facebook.com/notes/synapse-3di/3d-training-learning-collaboration-a-virtual-worlds-conference-live-from-dc/83612663001.

[18] M. Regan, "Diversity 2017: What Does the Future Hold?" *Profiles in Diversity Journal,* July/August 2007, retrieved June 20, 2010 at *www.diversityjournal.com/ee/pdj070708gja04/pdj070708gja04.pdf.*

[19] A. Derryberry, Interview with authors, 2009.

[20] B. Reeves, "How Video Games Build Leaders," On Leadership Video Transcript, *The Washington Post,* April 6, 2010, retrieved June 20, 2010 at http://www.washingtonpost.com/wp-dyn/content/video/2010/04/07/VI2010040701157.html.

[21] Hamilton, Interview.

[22] ASTD (American Society for Training & Development), *Transforming Learning with Web 2.0 Technologies,* Research Report (Alexandria, VA: ASTD Press, 2010).

[23] K. Kapp, Interview with authors, 2009.

[24] G. Schreck, Interview with authors, 2009.

[25] J. Miller, Interview with authors, 2009.

[26] Oehlert, Interview.

Chapter 7

[1] S. Kaplan, Interview with authors, 2009.

[2] J. Foner, Interview with authors, 2009.

[3] O. Mitchell, Interview with authors, 2009.

[4] R. Scoble, "Twitter and the Mark Zuckerberg Interview," *WebProNews*, March 11, 2008, retrieved June 20, 2010 at http://www.webpronews.com/blogtalk/2008/03/11/twitter-and-the-mark-zuckerberg-interview.

[5] Weber Shandwick, "2009 Global Five Star Events," a poll conducted by Weber Shandwick, January 26, 2009, retrieved July 13, 2010 at http://www.webershandwick.com/Default.aspx/AboutUs/PressReleases/2009/Business LeadershipConferencesStillInDemandandGrowingDespiteEconomicRecession AccordingtoNewWeberShandwickStudy.

[6] G. Koelling, Interview with authors, 2009.

[7] D. Sharesky, Interview with authors, 2009.

[8] R. Happe, Interview with authors, 2009.

[9] J. Veen, Interview with authors, 2009.

[10] L. Lawley, "Confessions of a Backchannel Queen," Mamamusings blog post, March 30, 2004, retrieved June 20, 2010 at http://mamamusings.net/archives/2004/03/30/confessions_of_a_backchannel_queen.php.

[11] L. Fitton, Interview with authors, 2009.

[12] Veen, Interview.

[13] P. Gillin, "While I Talked, People Twittered," Pistachio Consulting blog post, September 11, 2008, retrieved June 20, 2010 at http://pistachioconsulting.com/while-i-talked-people-twittered/.

[14] G. Brown-Martin, Interview with authors, 2009.

[15] T. Uhl, Interview with authors, 2009.

[16] To learn more about the process Tracy Hamilton used to create the DevLearn 2009 Conference Tweetbook, see http://discovery-thru-elearning.blogspot.com/2009/10/composing-tweetbook-for-devlearn-2009.html. To download the DevLearn 2009 Conference Tweetbook, visit http://www.elearningguild.com/content.cfm?selection=doc.1275.

[17] S. Berkun, *Confessions of a Public Speaker* (Sebastopol, CA: O'Reilly Media, 2009).

[18] J. Andrade, "What Does Doodling Do?" *Applied Cognitive Psychology* 24(1): 100-6.

[19] E. Eckman, Interview with authors, 2009.

[20] K. Hamlin, Interview with authors, 2009.

For Further Reading

Allen, D. *Getting Things Done: The Art of Stress-Free Productivity.* New York: Penguin, 2002.

Ben Betts Is Stoatly Different: A Stoatly Different eLearning Blog. http://www.ht2.org/ben/?paged=2.

Brogan, C. *Social Media 101: Tactics and Tips to Develop Your Business Online.* Hoboken, NJ: John Wiley & Sons, 2010.

Brogan, C. http://www.chrisbrogan.com.

Cross, J. *Informal Learning: Rediscovering the Natural Pathways that Inspire Innovation and Performance.* San Francisco: Pfeiffer, 2007.

Cross, J. *Working Smarter: Informal Learning in the Cloud.* Berkeley, CA: Internet Time Group, 2010.

Doug Engelbart Institute. http://dougengelbart.org.

Fitton, L., M. Gruen, and L. Poston. *Twitter for Dummies.* Indianapolis, IN: John Wiley & Sons, 2009.

Gillin, P. *Secrets of Social Media Marketing: How to Use Online Conversations and Customer Communities to Turbo-Charge Your Business!* Fresno, CA: Quill Driver Books, 2008.

Gillin, P. *The New Influencers: A Marketer's Guide to the New Social Media.* Fresno, CA: Linden, 2009.

Hagel, III, J., J. Seely Brown, and L. Davison. *The Power of Pull: How Small Moves, Smartly Made, Can Set Big Things in Motion.* Philadelphia, PA: Perseus Books, 2010.

Israel, S. *Twitterville: How Businesses Can Thrive in the New Global Neighborhoods.* New York: Portfolio, 2009.

Jean Piaget Society. http://www.piaget.org.

Lave, J., and E. Wenger. *Situated Learning: Legitimate Peripheral Participation.* Cambridge, UK: Cambridge University Press, 1991.

Li, C., and J. Bernoff. *Groundswell: Winning in a World Transformed by Social Technologies.* Boston: Harvard Business Press, 2008.

Light, R. The College Experience: A Blueprint for Success. Retrieved June 18, 2010 at http://athome.harvard.edu/programs/light/index.html.

Quinn, C. *mLearning.* San Francisco: Pfeiffer, 2010.

Rheingold, H. *Smart Mobs: The Next Social Revolution.* Cambridge, MA: Perseus Books Group, 2002.

Robbins, S., and M. Bell. *Second Life for Dummies.* Hoboken, NJ: John Wiley & Sons, 2008.

Rosenberg, M.J. *E-Learning: Strategies for Delivering Knowledge in the Digital Age.* New York: McGraw-Hill, 2001.

Rosenberg, M.J. *Beyond E-Learning: Approaches and Technologies to Enhance Organizational Knowledge, Learning, and Performance.* San Francisco: John Wiley & Sons, 2006.

Scoble, R., and S. Israel. *Naked Conversations: How Blogs Are Changing the Way Businesses Talk with Customers.* Hoboken, NJ: John Wiley & Sons, 2006.

Seely Brown, J., and P. Duguid. *The Social Life of Information.* Boston: Harvard Business School Press, 2000.

Shirky, C. *Here Comes Everybody: The Power of Organizing Without Organizations.* New York: Penguin Press, 2008.

Shirky, C. *Cognitive Surplus: Creativity and Generosity in a Connected Age.* New York: Penguin Press, 2010.

Solis, B. *Engage: The Complete Guide for Brands and Businesses to Build, Cultivate, and Measure Success in the New Web.* Hoboken, NJ: John Wiley & Sons, 2010.

Tapscott, D. *Grown Up Digital: How the Net Generation Is Changing Your World.* New York: McGraw-Hill, 2008.

Wenger, E. *Communities of Practice: Learning, Meaning, and Identity.* Cambridge, UK: Cambridge University Press, 1999.

Wenger, E., N. White, and J.D. Smith. *Digital Habitats: Stewarding Technology for Communities.* Portland, OR: CPSquare, 2009.

Yngve, V. On Getting a Word in Edgewise. Papers from the Sixth Regional Meeting [of the] Chicago Linguistic Society, 1970, p. 568.

About the Authors

Tony Bingham is the president and CEO of the American Society for Training & Development (ASTD), the world's largest professional association dedicated to the training and development field. ASTD offers programs and services to help members improve individual and organizational performance through learning. ASTD's 130 chapters in the United States and 30 international partners provide opportunities for members to convene at the local and regional levels throughout the world.

Together with the board of directors and supported by a staff of 90 and a wide volunteer network, Tony is focused on helping members lead talent management in their organizations, demonstrate positive business impact, understand the power of social media on informal learning, close skills gaps, and connect their work to the strategic priorities of business.

Tony coauthored *Presenting Learning: Ensure CEOs Get the Value of Learning*, a book to help learning professionals articulate the business case for learning more persuasively, position themselves as a strategic partner, and communicate a compelling story about the impact of learning on business results.

With broad-based business, financial, operational, and technical management expertise, Tony joined ASTD in 2001 as the chief operating officer / chief information officer. He became president and CEO in February 2004.

Marcia Conner is a partner at Altimeter Group, a research-based advisory firm that helps companies at a crossroads tackle the world's toughest business challenges. Working with organizations and industries to leverage disruption to their advantage, she applies experience from across disciplines to accelerate collaborative culture, workplace learning, and social business. She's a fellow at the Darden School of Business, founder of the popular Twitter chat #lrnchat, and writes the *Fast Company* column "Learn at All Levels."

Her expertise spans the most critical areas that drive sustainable success: leadership, strategy, technology, education, and design. Applied together she shows how engaging the brainpower of everyone in an organizational ecosystem can provide competitive advantage and strengthen the bottom line.

A 20-year veteran of the enterprise market, Marcia was vice president of education services and information futurist for PeopleSoft, senior manager of worldwide training at Microsoft, editor in chief of *Learning in the New Economy* magazine, and a fellow of the Society for New Communications Research.

She is also author of *Learn More Now*; coauthor of *Creating a Learning Culture: Strategy, Technology, and Practice*; and writes the Learnativity blog on the critical intersection among learning, creativity, activity, and productivity.

About the American Society for Training & Development

The American Society for Training & Development (ASTD) is the world's largest professional association dedicated to the training and development field. In more than 100 countries, ASTD's members work in organizations of all sizes, in the private and public sectors, as independent consultants, and as suppliers. Members connect locally in 130 U.S. chapters and with 30 international partners.

ASTD provides world-class professional development opportunities, content, networking, and resources for training and development professionals. Dedicated to helping members increase their relevance, enhance their skills, and align learning to organizational results, ASTD sets the standard for best practices within the profession.

ASTD started in 1943 and in recent years has widened the profession's focus to align learning and performance to organizational results, and is a sought-after voice on critical public policy issues. For more information visit www.astd.org.

About Berrett-Koehler Publishers

Berrett-Koehler is an independent publisher dedicated to an ambitious mission: Creating a World That Works for All.

We believe that to truly create a better world, action is needed at all levels—individual, organizational, and societal. At the individual level, our publications help people align their lives with their values and with their aspirations for a better world. At the organizational level, our publications promote progressive leadership and management practices, socially responsible approaches to business, and humane and effective organizations. At the societal level, our publications advance social and economic justice, shared prosperity, sustainability, and new solutions to national and global issues.

Visit Our Website

Go to www.bkconnection.com to read exclusive excerpts of new books, get special discounts, see videos of our authors, read their blogs, find out about author appearances and other BK events, browse our complete catalog, and more!

Get the *BK Communiqué,* Our Free eNewsletter

News about Berrett-Koehler, yes—new book announcements, special offers, author interviews. But also news by Berrett-Koehler authors, employees, and fellow travelers. Tales of the book trade. Links to our favorite websites and videos—informative, amusing, sometimes inexplicable. Trivia questions—win a free book! Letters to the editor. And much more! See a sample issue: www.bkconnection.com/BKCommunique.

Index